Unleashing Wealth: A Guide to BRRRR Real Estate Investing

Real Estate Investing, Volume 13

Jim Pellerin

Published by Jim Pellerin, 2024.

UNLEASHING WEALTH: A GUIDE TO BRRRR REAL ESTATE INVESTING

First edition. February 25, 2024.

ISBN: 979-8224373178

Written by Jim Pellerin.

Also by Jim Pellerin

Real Estate Investing

Real Estate Investing Strategies: The Secret to Financial Independence with Real Estate

Real Estate Investing with Lease Options - Investing in Real Estate with No Money Down

Invest Now - The Passive Approach to Winning at Real Estate

The Ultimate Beginners Guide to Real Estate Investing

The 98 Best Real Estate Investing Strategies

The Ultimate Beginners Guide to Wholesale Real Estate Investing

The Ultimate Beginners Guide to Rental Real Estate Investing

The Ultimate Beginners Guide to Fix and Flip Real Estate Investing

The Ultimate Beginners Guide to Private Equity Real Estate Investing

Ultimate Beginners Guide to Real Estate Investing Financing

Building Wealth Through Real Estate - A Beginners Retirement Guide

The Ultimate Guide to Marketing for Real Estate Investors

Unleashing Wealth: A Guide to BRRRR Real Estate Investing

Watch for more at www.jimpellerin.com.

Table of Contents

Unleashing Wealth

A Guide to

BRRRR

Real Estate Investing

Jim Pellerin

Updated for 2024

Chapter 1: Setting the Stage for Financial Freedom

Section 1: Definition of BRRRR Method

The world of real estate investing is dynamic and multifaceted, offering various strategies to those seeking financial freedom. Among these, the BRRRR method has emerged as a powerful and systematic approach, reshaping the landscape of real estate investment. In this section, we embark on a journey to explore the essence of the BRRRR method, providing a brief overview of its components—Buy, Rehab, Rent, Refinance, Repeat—and delving into why BRRRR stands out as a potent strategy for those aiming to build wealth through real estate.

Brief Overview of BRRRR: Buy, Rehab, Rent, Refinance, Repeat

At its core, the BRRRR method is an acronym that encapsulates a step-by-step real estate investment strategy. Each phase plays a distinct role in the overall process, creating a cyclical and repeatable framework for investors. Let's delve into each component of the BRRRR method:

Buy

The initial step in the BRRRR method involves purchasing a property strategically. Unlike traditional real estate strategies, where the focus may solely be on finding a property to hold or flip, BRRRR emphasizes a mindful approach to property acquisition. Investors seek properties with the potential for appreciation and positive cash flow.

Rehab (or Renovate)

Following the acquisition, the rehabilitation phase kicks in. Here, the investor strategically renovates and improves the property to enhance its value. The goal is not just to make the property aesthetically pleasing but to maximize its market value. The extent of renovations may vary, from cosmetic upgrades to comprehensive overhauls, depending on the investor's goals.

Rent

Once the property is renovated, the focus shifts to generating rental income. Renting out the property is a crucial step in the BRRRR method, as it provides a consistent cash flow that can offset expenses and contribute to the overall return on investment. The rental income generated during this phase is a key element in the financial success of the BRRRR strategy.

Refinance

The refinance phase is a strategic move to optimize the financial structure of the investment. By refinancing the property, investors can access the equity built through renovations and appreciation. This influx of capital allows for the repayment of initial investment funds and positions the investor to repeat the BRRRR cycle, using the refinanced property as leverage for additional investments.

Repeat

The beauty of the BRRRR method lies in its cyclical nature. After completing a full cycle, investors are not bound to stop; instead, they can repeat the entire process. The profits generated from one BRRRR cycle can be reinvested into another property, compounding the returns and progressively building a robust real estate portfolio.

Why BRRRR is a Powerful Real Estate Investment Strategy

The power of the BRRRR method lies in its ability to align with various financial goals and adapt to different market conditions. Here are key reasons why BRRRR stands out as a powerful real estate investment strategy.

Versatility

BRRRR is a versatile strategy that accommodates various investment goals. Whether an investor is seeking short-term gains through property flips or long-term wealth accumulation through rental income, the BRRRR method provides a flexible framework.

Risk Mitigation

By incorporating strategic property selection, due diligence, and renovation planning, BRRRR inherently includes risk mitigation measures. Thorough research and careful execution during each phase help minimize potential challenges, making it a prudent strategy for investors concerned about risk.

Leverage

The BRRRR method leverages the power of financing. Through the *refinance* phase, investors can access the equity built in the property without selling it. This ability to leverage existing assets allows for the efficient use of capital, magnifying the potential returns on investment.

Continuous Growth

The repeatable nature of the BRRRR method fosters continuous growth. As investors cycle through buy, rehab, rent, and refinance phases, they compound the returns and steadily build a portfolio of income-generating properties. This cyclical approach is conducive to long-term wealth creation.

Adaptability

Real estate markets are dynamic, and strategies that succeed in one economic climate may need adjustment in another. BRRRR's adaptability allows investors to navigate changing market conditions. Whether it's adjusting the level of renovations or refining the criteria for property selection, BRRRR accommodates strategic flexibility.

Equity Building

The BRRRR method is not just about generating immediate income; it's about building equity over time. Each phase contributes to the overall appreciation of the property, and the refinance phase enables investors to unlock that accumulated equity. This equity can then be used to finance additional investments or other financial goals.

Real-life Application and Case Studies

To illustrate the real-life application of the BRRRR method, let's explore a case study. Meet Sarah, an investor looking to build a diversified real estate portfolio for long-term wealth accumulation.

In the *buy* phase, Sarah strategically selects properties in emerging neighborhoods with growth potential. Through the *rehab* phase, she undertakes moderate renovations, focusing on improvements that yield the highest return on investment. *Renting* out the property provides a steady income stream during the rent phase, contributing to the property's overall return.

During the *refinance* phase, Sarah capitalizes on the increased property value and extracts equity. This newly acquired capital is then reinvested in additional properties during the *repeat* phase. Over time, Sarah compounds her returns, steadily building a portfolio of income-generating properties that align with her long-term financial goals.

Conclusion

The BRRRR method stands as a dynamic and powerful real estate investment strategy, offering investors a systematic approach to building wealth through property acquisition, rehabilitation, rental income, and strategic refinancing. Its versatility, risk mitigation measures, leverage opportunities, continuous growth potential, adaptability, and focus on equity building make it a compelling choice for those seeking financial freedom through real estate.

Section 2: The Journey to Financial Freedom

In the pursuit of financial freedom, the journey is often as transformative and enlightening as the destination itself. This section delves into the profound concept of the journey to financial freedom, exploring the mindset, strategies, and milestones that individuals navigate on their path to achieving economic independence. As we embark on this exploration, it's crucial to recognize that financial freedom is not merely a destination but a dynamic and evolving journey that intertwines with various aspects of life.

Defining Financial Freedom

Before delving into the journey, it's essential to define what financial freedom means. Financial freedom is a state where individuals have the resources, assets, and financial security to make life choices without being constrained by monetary concerns. It involves achieving a level of financial independence that allows individuals to pursue their passions, goals, and desired lifestyle without the perpetual burden of financial stress.

Breaking Free from Financial Constraints

Financial freedom involves breaking free from the constraints that hinder one's ability to live life on their terms. This liberation is not solely about accumulating wealth but also about establishing financial stability, cultivating a mindset of abundance, and creating avenues for sustained prosperity.

The Interconnected Nature of Financial Freedom

Financial freedom extends beyond the numerical values on bank statements. It intertwines with personal values, life aspirations, and the pursuit of happiness. The journey to financial freedom is a holistic endeavor that addresses both the tangible and intangible aspects of a fulfilling and abundant life.

The Mindset of Financial Freedom

Embarking on the journey to financial freedom necessitates a shift in mindset – a transition from a scarcity mindset to one of abundance and possibility. Here are key elements of the mindset conducive to the journey:

Goal Clarity

Individuals on the path to financial freedom possess clarity about their goals. Whether it's buying a home, starting a business, or funding education, having well-defined objectives provides direction and purpose to financial decisions.

Long-Term Vision

Financial freedom is a journey that unfolds over time. Individuals with a long-term vision understand that the journey involves strategic planning, disciplined execution, and a commitment to continuous improvement.

Embracing Learning

The journey to financial freedom is an educational process. Those on this journey embrace learning opportunities, seeking knowledge about personal finance, investment strategies, and wealth-building principles.

Resilience and Adaptability

Challenges are inevitable on the path to financial freedom. A resilient mindset enables individuals to navigate setbacks, learn from failures, and adapt their strategies to changing circumstances.

Strategies for the Journey

The journey to financial freedom is not a one-size-fits-all experience. However, there are foundational strategies that can guide individuals on their path to economic independence.

Budgeting and Financial Planning

Creating a budget and developing a financial plan are fundamental steps. Budgeting allows individuals to allocate resources wisely, save for future goals, and curb unnecessary expenses. A comprehensive financial plan provides a roadmap for achieving milestones on the journey.

Debt Management

Effectively managing and reducing debt is a critical strategy on the journey to financial freedom. Individuals focus on paying off high-interest debts, consolidating loans when beneficial, and adopting responsible credit practices.

Income Diversification

Diversifying income sources provides stability and resilience. Individuals explore avenues for additional income, such as side businesses, investments, or passive income streams, to build financial security.

Strategic Investments

Investing intelligently is a key aspect of the journey. Individuals educate themselves on investment opportunities, diversify their portfolios, and consider long-term wealth-building instruments like real estate.

Emergency Fund

Establishing an emergency fund is a safety net on the journey to financial freedom. This fund provides a financial buffer during unexpected expenses or periods of income instability, preventing setbacks in the overall journey.

Milestones on the Journey

The journey to financial freedom is marked by significant milestones, each representing a step closer to economic independence. While individual milestones may vary, common markers on this transformative journey include:

Achieving Debt Freedom

Paying off debts, especially high-interest ones, is a substantial milestone. Individuals experience a sense of liberation and increased financial flexibility as they eliminate debt burdens.

Building an Emergency Fund

The establishment of a robust emergency fund signifies a heightened level of financial security. It serves as a financial cushion, shielding individuals from unforeseen circumstances.

Homeownership

For many, owning a home is a symbolic and tangible milestone on the journey to financial freedom. It represents stability, an asset, and a place to call one's own.

Investment Portfolio Growth

Watching an investment portfolio grow is a tangible indicator of progress. Individuals witness the compounding effect of strategic investments as their wealth accumulates over time.

Passive Income Streams

Generating passive income streams, such as rental income from real estate investments, dividends from stocks, or royalties from intellectual property, represents a shift towards financial freedom. Passive income provides financial autonomy and the ability to support one's lifestyle without active employment.

Early Retirement or Financial Independence

Attaining the ability to retire early or achieve financial independence is the ultimate destination on the journey to financial freedom. It means having the choice to work for fulfillment rather than necessity.

Real-life Application and Case Studies

To provide a tangible illustration of the journey to financial freedom, let's explore a real-life case study. Meet Sarah, a professional in her mid-30s with a vision for financial independence.

Sarah's Journey

1. **Goal Setting:** Sarah begins her journey by setting clear financial goals. These include paying off student loans, establishing an emergency fund, and investing for future financial security.

2. **Budgeting and Debt Repayment:** Sarah creates a budget that allocates a portion of her income to debt repayment. She adopts a disciplined approach, allocating extra funds to eliminate high-interest debts systematically.
3. **Emergency Fund:** As Sarah achieves debt freedom, she prioritizes building an emergency fund. This fund serves as a financial safety net, providing peace of mind and protection against unforeseen expenses.
4. **Strategic Investments:** Sarah educates herself on investment strategies and begins strategically investing in a diversified portfolio. She explores real estate as a long-term wealth-building avenue due to its potential for passive income and property appreciation.
5. **Passive Income Generation:** As Sarah's real estate investments mature, she starts generating passive income through rental properties. This income contributes to her financial independence, allowing her to have more flexibility in her career choices.
6. **Financial Independence:** By her early 40s, Sarah achieves financial independence. She has the freedom to choose whether to continue working, pursue passion projects, or retire early. The journey transforms her mindset, providing a sense of empowerment and fulfillment.

Conclusion

The journey to financial freedom is a transformative and empowering endeavor that extends beyond the realm of monetary gains. It encompasses mindset shifts, strategic planning, and the achievement of significant milestones. Recognizing financial freedom as a dynamic journey, individuals can embark on a path that aligns with their values, aspirations, and desired lifestyle.

Section 3: The Target Audience

The journey to financial freedom is not a one-size-fits-all endeavor, and similarly, the BRRRR real estate investing method caters to a diverse audience seeking financial independence. In this section, we explore the target audience for BRRRR investing, identifying those who can benefit the most from this powerful real estate investment strategy. Additionally, we dispel common myths surrounding real estate investing, providing clarity for prospective investors and demystifying any misconceptions that may hinder their journey to financial freedom.

Who Can Benefit from BRRRR Investing?

The BRRRR method is a versatile and adaptive strategy that can be harnessed by a broad spectrum of individuals. Whether you're a novice investor taking your first steps into the world of real estate or a seasoned professional looking to optimize your portfolio, BRRRR offers a strategic framework for achieving financial goals. Here's a closer look at the diverse range of individuals who can benefit from BRRRR investing:

1. **New Investors**

- *Why BRRRR?* New investors benefit from the structured and sequential nature of the BRRRR method. It provides a step-by-step guide, simplifying the complex world of real estate investment for those just starting.
- *Dispelling Myths:* New investors often face myths that real estate is exclusively for the wealthy or experienced. BRRRR dispels this myth by offering a systematic approach that allows individuals to start with smaller investments and grow over time.

2. **Experienced Investors**

- *Why BRRRR?* Experienced investors appreciate the scalability of the BRRRR method. It allows them to leverage their existing knowledge and resources to execute larger and more complex real estate transactions.
- *Dispelling Myths:* Some experienced investors may harbor doubts about the feasibility of consistently repeating successful real estate transactions. BRRRR, with its focus on repetition, challenges this myth by providing a systematic and scalable approach.

3. **Entrepreneurs**

- *Why BRRRR?* Entrepreneurs seeking to diversify their investment portfolio find BRRRR appealing due to its alignment with an entrepreneurial mindset. It requires strategic thinking, adaptability, and a willingness to take calculated risks.
- *Dispelling Myths:* Entrepreneurs may hesitate to invest in real estate due to perceived complexities. BRRRR dispels the myth that real estate is overly complicated by offering a structured and repeatable process.

4. **Passive Income Seekers**

- *Why BRRRR?* Individuals aiming to generate consistent passive income appreciate the rent phase of the BRRRR method. It provides a systematic approach to property management, facilitating steady cash flow.
- *Dispelling Myths:* Some may believe that managing rental properties is too time-consuming or stressful. BRRRR challenges this myth by emphasizing strategic property selection, renovations, and professional property

management.

5. **Individuals with Limited Capital**

- *Why BRRRR?* BRRRR is accessible to individuals with limited capital due to its focus on leveraging borrowed funds and the potential for refinancing to extract equity. It allows investors to maximize returns with relatively modest initial investments.
- *Dispelling Myths:* Limited capital is often seen as a barrier to real estate investing. BRRRR dispels this myth by providing strategies to leverage resources intelligently and grow investments over time.

Dispelling Common Myths about Real Estate Investing

To create a clear path for potential investors, it's crucial to dispel common myths that may act as barriers to entry or hinder the adoption of real estate investing strategies. Let's address and dispel some of these prevalent misconceptions:

1. **Myth: Real Estate is Only for the Wealthy:**

- *Reality:* While it's true that real estate can be a substantial investment, the BRRRR method allows individuals to start with smaller properties and grow their portfolio over time. It leverages borrowed funds, making it accessible to a wider range of investors.

2. **Myth: Real Estate Investing is Too Complex:**

- *Reality:* BRRRR simplifies the real estate investing process by breaking it down into distinct phases. It provides a structured approach, making it manageable even for those with limited experience.

3. **Myth: Real Estate Requires Active Involvement:**

- *Reality:* BRRRR acknowledges the varying levels of involvement investors may desire. Whether seeking active management for higher returns or opting for a more hands-off approach with professional property management, BRRRR accommodates different preferences.

4. **Myth: Real Estate is Risky:**

- *Reality:* Every investment carries some level of risk, but BRRRR emphasizes risk management strategies. Thorough due diligence, diversification, and contingency planning are integral components of the BRRRR method.

5. **Myth: Real Estate is Illiquid:**

- *Reality:* While real estate is a relatively illiquid asset, the BRRRR method introduces a degree of liquidity through refinancing. Investors can extract equity from properties, providing capital for future investments or addressing liquidity needs.

6. **Myth: Real Estate is Not for Young Investors:**

- *Reality:* BRRRR challenges the myth that real estate is not suitable for younger investors. Its systematic approach allows individuals to start building wealth early, setting the stage for long-term financial success.

Conclusion

Understanding the diverse audience that can benefit from BRRRR investing is pivotal in democratizing access to financial freedom through real estate. The BRRRR method offers a structured and scalable approach that resonates with both new and experienced investors, entrepreneurs, passive income seekers, and individuals with limited capital. By dispelling common myths about real estate investing, we pave the way for a broader audience to embark on the transformative journey to financial freedom.

Section 4: Outline of the Book

As we embark on this journey towards financial freedom through the powerful BRRRR real estate investing method, it's essential to provide a roadmap that guides readers through the key insights and strategies. In this section, we present an overview of the ten chapters that constitute this book, offering a glimpse into the rich content that awaits. Each chapter is designed to build a comprehensive understanding of the BRRRR method, from its foundational principles to its practical application and the intricacies of successful real estate investing. Let's explore what readers can expect from each section of the book.

Chapter 1: Introduction Chapter

Setting the Stage for Financial Freedom: Establishing the context for the book, this chapter introduces the concept of financial freedom and how the BRRRR method serves as a powerful tool in achieving it.

Chapter 2: Goals Chapter - Building Your Blueprint for Success

Defining Financial Goals: This chapter guides readers in identifying short-term and long-term financial objectives and explores how the BRRRR method aligns with these goals.

Chapter 3: Buy Chapter - Laying the Foundation

Strategic Property Acquisition: This chapter focuses on the initial step of the BRRRR method – buying properties strategically to maximize returns.

Chapter 4: Rehab Chapter - Enhancing Property Value

Maximizing Property Potential: This chapter delves into the rehabilitation phase, where strategic renovations enhance property value.

Chapter 5: Rent Chapter - Generating Steady Income

Unlocking Rental Potential: This chapter focuses on the rent phase, where the property transforms into a source of steady income.

Chapter 6: Refinance Chapter - Maximizing Property Value

Optimizing Property Value Through Refinancing: This chapter explores the refinance phase, where investors extract equity for future investments or to address financial goals.

Chapter 7: Repeat Chapter - Compound Growth in Action

Building Wealth Through Repetition: This chapter emphasizes the cyclical and repetitive nature of the BRRRR method, showcasing how compound growth unfolds over multiple cycles.

Chapter 8: Risks Chapter - Navigating Challenges

Proactive Risk Management: This chapter focuses on understanding potential challenges in real estate investing and strategies for mitigating risks.

Chapter 9: Scaling Chapter - Growing Your Portfolio

Strategies for Portfolio Expansion: This chapter explores avenues for scaling real estate investments and growing a robust and diversified portfolio.

Chapter 10: Conclusions Chapter

Reflecting on the Journey: This concluding chapter summarizes key insights, recaps the BRRRR method's power, and encourages readers to apply their newfound knowledge.

What to Expect from Each Section

Throughout the book, readers can expect a balance between theoretical knowledge and practical application. Each section provides a thorough exploration of its respective topic, accompanied by real-life examples, case studies, and actionable insights.

The book aims to empower readers with the knowledge and confidence to embark on their own journey to financial freedom through the BRRRR method. Whether you are a novice investor, an experienced professional, or someone in between, each chapter offers valuable insights and practical guidance to help you navigate the complexities of real estate investing and unlock the doors to economic independence.

Chapter 2: Goals - Building Your Blueprint for Success

Section 1: Identifying Financial Goals

In the journey towards financial freedom, the first crucial step is to identify clear and achievable financial goals. This section of the Goals Chapter explores the significance of setting both short-term and long-term objectives. Additionally, we delve into how the BRRRR real estate investing method aligns with these goals, providing a powerful blueprint for success.

The Importance of Identifying Financial Goals

1. **Clarity and Direction**

- Setting financial goals provides clarity and direction in one's financial journey. It transforms abstract desires into tangible objectives, guiding decision-making and resource allocation.

2. **Motivation and Purpose**

- Defined goals serve as powerful motivators, offering a sense of purpose and fueling the determination required to overcome challenges. They create a vision for the future that propels individuals towards financial success.

3. **Resource Allocation**

- Financial goals help allocate resources wisely. Whether it's saving for a down payment, investing for retirement, or creating an emergency fund, each goal dictates a specific allocation of time, effort, and funds.

4. **Measuring Progress**

- Goals provide measurable benchmarks for progress. Regularly assessing achievements against these benchmarks allows individuals to track their financial journey and make informed adjustments as needed.

5. **Risk Mitigation**

- Clearly defined goals contribute to effective risk management. They enable individuals to assess potential risks in relation to their objectives, allowing for the implementation of proactive strategies to mitigate risks.

Short-term and Long-term Financial Objectives

1. **Short-term Objectives**

- Short-term financial goals typically cover a period of one year or less. These objectives are often stepping stones towards larger, long-term goals. Examples include building an emergency fund, paying off high-interest debts, or saving for a specific purchase.
- *How BRRRR Aligns:* The BRRRR method aligns with short-term goals by providing a structured and sequential approach. The buy and rehab phases, in particular, can yield relatively quick results in terms of property acquisition and value enhancement.

2. **Long-term Objectives**

- Long-term financial goals extend beyond the one-year horizon and often involve substantial achievements. Examples include funding education, purchasing a home, achieving retirement security, or building generational wealth.
- *How BRRRR Aligns:* The BRRRR method aligns with long-term goals by offering a repeatable and scalable framework. Through strategic repetition, investors can accumulate properties, generate passive income, and build substantial equity over time.

How BRRRR Aligns with Financial Goals

1. **Building Wealth Through Property Appreciation**

- *Short-term Goal Alignment:* The buy phase of the BRRRR method involves strategic property acquisition, aligning with the short-term goal of building a real estate portfolio. Property appreciation, a key component of wealth building, can begin relatively quickly.
- *Long-term Goal Alignment:* Property appreciation continues to contribute to long-term wealth building. Over multiple BRRRR cycles, investors witness exponential growth in property values, aligning with the objective of achieving substantial financial milestones.

2. **Generating Passive Income Through Renting**

- *Short-term Goal Alignment:* The rent phase of BRRRR focuses on transforming the property into a source of steady income, aligning with the short-term goal of generating passive income. Rental income provides an immediate return on investment.

- *Long-term Goal Alignment:* The rent phase contributes to long-term passive income generation. As investors repeat the BRRRR cycle, the cumulative effect of rental income from multiple properties aligns with the objective of creating sustained financial independence.

3. **Optimizing Capital Through Refinancing**

- *Short-term Goal Alignment:* Refinancing, a critical component of the BRRRR method, aligns with short-term goals by providing the opportunity to optimize capital. Extracting equity through refinancing can fund additional investments or address immediate financial needs.
- *Long-term Goal Alignment:* The ability to strategically extract equity from properties supports long-term financial objectives. Whether funding education, purchasing additional properties, or achieving other milestones, refinancing aligns with a dynamic and evolving financial plan.

4. **Cyclical and Repeatable Growth**

- *Short-term Goal Alignment:* The cyclical nature of the BRRRR method offers short-term growth through each completed cycle. Investors can quickly see returns on their initial investment as properties are renovated and rented.
- *Long-term Goal Alignment:* The BRRRR method's repeatability aligns with the long-term goal of building a scalable real estate portfolio. Through strategic repetition, investors compound their wealth, achieving financial milestones over the course of multiple cycles.

Real-life Application and Case Studies

To illustrate how BRRRR aligns with financial goals, let's explore a real-life case study. Meet James, a new investor with a goal to build a diversified real estate portfolio.

James's Financial Goal

1. **Short-term Goal:** Build a real estate portfolio with two properties within the next 12 months.
    - *BRRRR Alignment:* James adopts the BRRRR method, strategically selecting properties for quick renovation and renting. The cyclical nature of BRRRR allows him to achieve his short-term goal by completing two cycles within the desired timeframe.
2. **Long-term Goal:** Achieve financial independence through a portfolio of income-generating properties.
    - *BRRRR Alignment:* James recognizes the power of the BRRRR method's repetition. Over the next decade, he strategically repeats the BRRRR cycle, accumulating properties, generating passive income, and achieving long-term financial independence.

Conclusion

Identifying financial goals is the foundational step in the journey towards financial freedom. Whether short-term or long-term, these goals provide a roadmap, guiding individuals towards success. The BRRRR real estate investing method serves as a powerful tool that aligns seamlessly with these goals. Through strategic property acquisition, renovation, rental income generation, and cyclical repetition, BRRRR empowers investors to achieve both short-term milestones and long-term financial independence.

Section 2: Creating a Realistic Timeline

In the pursuit of financial freedom through real estate investing, creating a realistic timeline is a fundamental aspect of building a successful blueprint. This section explores the intricacies of setting achievable milestones and emphasizes the importance of patience in the realm of real estate investing. By understanding the dynamics of time in the context of financial goals, investors can navigate the journey with a clear sense of direction and the resilience needed for long-term success.

Setting Achievable Milestones

1. **Definition of Milestones**

    - Milestones are significant markers or achievements that denote progress towards a larger goal. In real estate investing, milestones can vary widely, from acquiring the first property to achieving a certain level of passive income.

2. **Importance of Milestones**

    - Milestones provide a tangible way to measure progress and celebrate achievements along the journey. They break down larger objectives into manageable and motivating steps, contributing to a sense of accomplishment.

3. **Aligning with Financial Goals**

    - Each milestone should be directly aligned with specific financial goals. Whether it's reaching a certain number of properties in a portfolio, achieving a target rental income, or successfully completing a renovation project, milestones should be tailored to an individual's overarching objectives.

4. **Flexibility and Adaptability**

- While milestones provide a structured framework, it's crucial to be flexible and adaptable. Real estate markets, economic conditions, and personal circumstances can evolve, requiring adjustments to timelines and milestones.

The Importance of Patience in Real Estate Investing

1. **Understanding the Real Estate Cycle**

- Real estate operates within cyclical patterns influenced by economic factors, market trends, and other external variables. Patience is essential as investors navigate through market fluctuations, understanding that opportunities may arise during various phases of the cycle.

2. **Long-term Wealth Building**

- Real estate investing, particularly through strategies like the BRRRR method, is a long-term wealth-building endeavor. Patience is a virtue as investors wait for property values to appreciate, rental income to compound, and the compounding effect of strategic repetition to manifest over time.

3. **Navigating Market Fluctuations**

- Real estate markets are dynamic, experiencing both periods of growth and downturns. Patience becomes a valuable asset during market downturns, allowing investors to weather the storm, hold onto valuable assets, and potentially capitalize on opportunities when the market rebounds.

4. **Risk Mitigation**

- Patience is intertwined with risk mitigation. Rushed decisions and impatience can lead to suboptimal choices. Patient investors take the time to conduct thorough due diligence, assess risks, and make informed decisions that align with their long-term goals.

Creating a Realistic Timeline with BRRRR

1. **Buy Phase Timeline**

- In the buy phase of the BRRRR method, patience is exercised during property selection and acquisition. This phase involves thorough market analysis, property research, and negotiations. Setting a realistic timeline ensures that investors do not compromise on due diligence in their eagerness to secure a property.

2. **Rehab Phase Timeline**

- Patience is crucial in the rehab phase as renovations are conducted. Rushed renovations may lead to subpar results or increased costs. A realistic timeline allows for careful planning, effective project management, and the execution of renovations that enhance property value.

3. **Rent Phase Timeline**

- The rent phase involves patience in setting rental prices, selecting tenants, and ensuring property maintenance. Rushed decisions may lead to suboptimal rental income or tenant-related challenges. A well-thought-out timeline ensures strategic decision-making for long-term income stability.

4. **Refinance Phase Timeline**

- During the refinance phase, patience is exercised in understanding market conditions and optimizing mortgage terms. A realistic timeline allows for the strategic extraction of equity without succumbing to external pressures. Patient refinancing contributes to long-term financial efficiency.

Real-life Application and Case Studies

To illustrate the importance of creating a realistic timeline and exercising patience in real estate investing, let's explore a real-life case study. Meet Sarah, an investor with a goal of building a diversified real estate portfolio over the next decade.

Sarah's Realistic Timeline

1. **Short-term Milestone (Year 1-2)**
    - *Goal:* Acquire two properties and complete the first BRRRR cycle.
    - *Timeline:* Sarah sets a realistic timeline of one to two years for her initial milestone, considering market conditions, property availability, and the time required for renovations and tenant placement.
2. **Intermediate Milestone (Year 3-5)**
    - *Goal:* Achieve a portfolio of five properties with consistent rental income.
    - *Timeline:* Recognizing the cyclical nature of real estate and allowing for strategic repetition, Sarah sets an intermediate milestone of three to five years. This timeline accommodates property acquisition, renovations, and the stabilization of rental income.
3. **Long-term Milestone (Year 10)**

  - *Goal:* Attain financial independence through a portfolio generating substantial passive income.
  - *Timeline:* Sarah's long-term milestone aligns with a ten-year timeline, understanding that the compounding effect of the BRRRR method takes time. This patient approach allows for the accumulation of properties, consistent rental income, and the optimization of equity through refinancing.

Conclusion

Creating a realistic timeline and exercising patience are pivotal components of a successful real estate investment journey. Milestones provide measurable markers of progress, aligning with specific financial goals. Patience, on the other hand, is the cornerstone of long-term wealth building, risk mitigation, and navigating the dynamic landscape of real estate markets.

In the context of the BRRRR method, a realistic timeline ensures strategic decision-making in each phase of the process. From property acquisition to renovations, tenant placement, and refinancing, each step requires careful consideration and patience to maximize returns and achieve long-term financial success.

Section 3: Risk Management

In the dynamic world of real estate investing, understanding and effectively managing risks are critical components of building a successful blueprint for financial freedom. This section explores the nuances of risk management, including the identification of potential challenges and the implementation of strategies to mitigate these risks. By proactively addressing uncertainties, investors can navigate the real estate landscape with confidence and resilience. Risks will also be covered in more detail in Chapter 9.

Understanding Potential Challenges in Real Estate Investing

1. **Market Risks**

- *Challenge:* Real estate markets are subject to fluctuations influenced by economic conditions, interest rates, and local factors. Changes in market trends can impact property values and rental income.
- *Understanding:* Investors need to stay informed about market trends, economic indicators, and local dynamics. Recognizing the cyclical nature of real estate markets allows for strategic decision-making in response to changing conditions.

2. **Operational Risks**

- *Challenge:* Managing properties comes with operational challenges, including unexpected maintenance issues, tenant turnover, and property management complexities.
- *Understanding:* Investors should anticipate and plan for operational challenges. Engaging professional property management services can streamline operations and address issues promptly, minimizing disruptions and preserving the value of the investment.

3. **Financial Risks**

- *Challenge:* Financial risks in real estate investing include interest rate fluctuations, unexpected expenses, and challenges in securing favorable financing.
- *Understanding:* Investors must conduct thorough financial

analysis and stress testing. Maintaining liquidity, exploring fixed-rate financing options, and having contingency funds can mitigate the impact of financial uncertainties.

4. **Legal and Regulatory Risks**

- *Challenge:* Legal and regulatory challenges can arise from changes in zoning laws, tenant rights, and compliance issues.
- *Understanding:* Staying informed about local regulations and seeking legal counsel when needed is crucial. Thorough due diligence on property-related legal aspects helps investors navigate potential legal challenges.

Strategies for Mitigating Risks in Real Estate Investing

1. **Diversification**

- *Strategy:* Diversifying the real estate portfolio across different property types and locations helps mitigate market-specific risks. A diverse portfolio is less vulnerable to the impact of localized economic downturns.
- *Application:* Investors can strategically choose properties in different neighborhoods or cities, ensuring that the overall portfolio is not overly reliant on the performance of a single market.

2. **Insurance Coverage**

- *Strategy:* Adequate insurance coverage is a fundamental risk mitigation strategy. Insurance policies can protect against property damage, liability claims, and other unforeseen events.
- *Application:* Investors should work with insurance

professionals to tailor coverage to the specific risks associated with their properties. Regular reviews of insurance policies ensure ongoing relevance and adequacy of coverage.

3. **Thorough Due Diligence**

- *Strategy:* Conducting thorough due diligence before property acquisition is a proactive approach to risk management. This includes comprehensive property inspections, title searches, and analysis of local market conditions.
- *Application:* Investors should invest time and resources in comprehensive research. Engaging professionals, such as inspectors and real estate attorneys, contributes to a well-informed decision-making process.

4. **Financial Contingency Planning**

- *Strategy:* Maintaining financial reserves for unforeseen expenses and market downturns is a prudent risk mitigation strategy. Having contingency funds provides a buffer against unexpected challenges.
- *Application:* Investors should allocate a portion of their budget for unforeseen expenses and market uncertainties. This financial cushion enhances resilience and minimizes the impact of unexpected financial challenges.

5. **Professional Property Management**

- *Strategy:* Engaging professional property management services can mitigate operational risks. Property managers handle day-to-day operations, tenant interactions, and maintenance, reducing the burden on individual investors.

- *Application:* Investors can research and select reputable property management firms with a proven track record. Clear communication and regular updates with property managers ensure a collaborative approach to risk mitigation.

6. **Continuous Education and Market Monitoring**

- *Strategy:* Staying informed about industry trends, legal changes, and market dynamics is essential for risk management. Continuous education allows investors to adapt to evolving conditions.
- *Application:* Investors should allocate time for ongoing learning, attend industry events, and stay connected with real estate networks. Regularly monitoring market conditions enables timely adjustments to investment strategies.

Real-life Application and Case Studies

To illustrate the practical application of risk management strategies in real estate investing, let's explore a case study. Meet Alex, an investor who navigates potential challenges through proactive risk management.

Alex's Risk Management Strategies

1. **Diversification**
    - *Challenge:* Alex is concerned about market-specific risks impacting property values.
    - *Strategy:* Alex diversifies his portfolio by investing in properties in different neighborhoods and cities.
    - *Outcome:* The diversified portfolio helps mitigate the impact of a localized economic downturn, as properties in other markets may continue to perform

well.

2. **Insurance Coverage**
    - *Challenge:* Alex worries about potential property damage or liability claims.
    - *Strategy:* Alex reviews and enhances his insurance coverage to adequately protect against various risks.
    - *Outcome:* In the event of unexpected events such as natural disasters or accidents, Alex's insurance coverage provides financial protection, minimizing potential losses.
3. **Thorough Due Diligence**
    - *Challenge:* Alex faces uncertainty about a property's condition and legal aspects.
    - *Strategy:* Alex conducts thorough due diligence, including property inspections and legal assessments.
    - *Outcome:* With comprehensive information, Alex makes an informed decision, avoiding potential pitfalls and ensuring the property aligns with his investment goals.
4. **Financial Contingency Planning:**
    - *Challenge:* Alex anticipates unexpected expenses or market downturns.
    - *Strategy:* Alex allocates a portion of his budget as a financial reserve for contingencies.
    - *Outcome:* When faced with unforeseen expenses or economic uncertainties, Alex has financial reserves to address challenges without compromising his overall financial stability.
5. **Professional Property Management**
    - *Challenge:* Alex is concerned about the operational complexities of managing multiple properties.

- *Strategy:* Alex engages professional property management services.
- *Outcome:* Property managers handle day-to-day operations, ensuring efficient management, tenant satisfaction, and timely resolution of issues.

Conclusion

Effective risk management is a cornerstone of successful real estate investing. By understanding potential challenges and implementing proactive strategies to mitigate risks, investors can safeguard their investments and navigate the dynamic real estate landscape with confidence.

Section 4: The Power of Compound Growth

In the pursuit of financial freedom through real estate investing, understanding the power of compound growth is akin to unlocking a secret pathway to exponential returns. This section delves into the profound impact of compound growth within the context of the BRRRR real estate investing method. By leveraging the cyclical and repetitive nature of BRRRR, investors can not only maximize returns on individual properties but also create a compounding effect that propels them toward their financial future.

Leveraging the BRRRR Method for Exponential Returns

1. **Sequential and Cyclical Nature of BRRRR**

- The BRRRR method, encompassing Buy, Rehab, Rent, Refinance, Repeat, operates in a sequential and cyclical manner. This unique structure sets the stage for compound growth as each cycle builds upon the previous one.

2. **Appreciation and Equity Accumulation**

    - Property appreciation and the strategic extraction of equity during the refinance phase contribute to compound growth. The increased equity from each cycle becomes a powerful financial resource for subsequent investments.

3. **Increasing Rental Income**

    - With each repetition of the BRRRR cycle, the investor adds another property to the portfolio. This not only multiplies the potential for property appreciation but also increases the overall rental income generated from the expanding portfolio.

4. **Optimizing Returns Through Repetition**

    - The repetition of the BRRRR method is key to unlocking compound growth. Investors strategically repeat the cycle, compounding their returns with each iteration. The compounding effect accelerates as the portfolio expands over time.

Visualizing Your Financial Future

1. **Setting Clear Financial Goals**

    - As discussed, visualizing your financial future begins with setting clear and measurable financial goals. These goals serve as the destination on your journey and provide a roadmap for the application of compound growth strategies.

2. **Understanding the Long-Term Impact**

    - Compound growth is a long-term phenomenon.

Understanding the impact of compounding over time encourages investors to adopt a patient and strategic approach to real estate investing.

3. **Strategic Repetition for Wealth Building**

- Visualizing your financial future involves recognizing the wealth-building potential of strategic repetition. Each repetition of the BRRRR cycle contributes to the compounding of wealth, propelling investors closer to their financial goals.

4. **Building a Scalable Portfolio**

- The power of compound growth is fully realized when investors build a scalable real estate portfolio. The scalability of the BRRRR method allows investors to continually add properties to their portfolio, multiplying the effects of compound growth.

The Mathematics of Compound Growth

1. **Exponential Increase in Property Value**

- Compound growth results in an exponential increase in property values. As properties appreciate in value, the equity accumulated in each property multiplies, contributing to an ever-growing financial foundation.

2. **Multiplying Rental Income**

- The compounding effect extends to rental income. With each property added to the portfolio, the overall rental income multiplies. This creates a diversified and robust income stream that supports ongoing investments.

3. **Accelerated Wealth Accumulation**

- Compound growth accelerates wealth accumulation. The strategic repetition of the BRRRR method ensures that the wealth generated from each cycle is reinvested, compounding the returns and fostering a cycle of accelerated growth.

4. **Optimizing Returns through Refinancing**

- Refinancing is a crucial element of the compound growth equation. Extracting equity through refinancing allows investors to optimize returns, providing additional capital for future investments and contributing to the compounding effect.

Real-life Application and Case Studies

To illustrate the practical application of compound growth through the BRRRR method, let's explore a case study. Meet Emily, an investor who strategically leverages compound growth for her financial future.

Emily's Compound Growth Strategy

1. **Initial BRRRR Cycle (Year 1)**
   - *Goal:* Acquire and renovate the first property using the BRRRR method.
   - *Outcome:* Emily completes her first BRRRR cycle, adding a property to her portfolio. The property appreciates, and Emily strategically extracts equity through refinancing.
2. **Second BRRRR Cycle (Year 2-3)**
   - *Goal:* Repeat the BRRRR cycle with the profits from

the first property.

- *Outcome:* Emily reinvests the profits from the first cycle into a second property. The portfolio now consists of two properties, and the cumulative equity and rental income increase.

3. **Strategic Repetition (Year 4-7)**
   - *Goal:* Continue strategic repetition of the BRRRR method.
   - *Outcome:* Over the next four years, Emily strategically repeats the BRRRR cycle, adding a property each year. The compounding effect accelerates as each property appreciates in value, and the overall rental income multiplies.
4. **Portfolio Expansion and Financial Freedom (Year 10)**
   - *Goal:* Achieve financial freedom through a diversified and scalable real estate portfolio.
   - *Outcome:* By year ten, Emily has built a portfolio of six properties through strategic repetition of the BRRRR method. The compound growth has resulted in substantial equity, diversified rental income, and financial freedom.

Conclusion

The power of compound growth, when harnessed through the strategic application of the BRRRR method, is a game-changer in the realm of real estate investing. Investors who grasp the sequential and cyclical nature of BRRRR, understand the mathematics of compound growth, and visualize their financial future can unlock exponential returns and build substantial wealth over time.

Chapter 3: Buy - The First Step in BRRRR Investing

Section 1: Market Research

Embarking on the BRRRR real estate investing journey begins with the foundational step of acquiring properties strategically. This section, the first part of the *Buy* stage, explores the critical aspect of market research. Successful BRRRR investors understand the importance of choosing the right location and analyzing market trends and demand. By conducting thorough market research, investors can make informed decisions that lay the groundwork for successful BRRRR cycles.

Choosing the Right Location

1. **Alignment with Investment Goals**

- The right location is one that aligns with the investor's overall investment goals. Whether the aim is for steady rental income, long-term appreciation, or a balance of both, the location should support these objectives.

2. **Demographic Considerations**

- Understanding the demographics of a location is crucial. Factors such as population growth, age distribution, and income levels influence the demand for rental properties and property values.

3. **Proximity to Amenities and Services**

- Properties located in proximity to essential amenities, schools, healthcare facilities, and public services tend to attract tenants. Access to conveniences enhances the property's appeal and potential for long-term demand.

4. **Market Stability and Resilience**

- Stability and resilience in the local real estate market are key considerations. Markets with consistent demand, low volatility, and economic stability provide a favorable environment for successful BRRRR investments.

Analyzing Market Trends and Demand

1. **Current Market Conditions**

- Understanding the current state of the real estate market is essential. Factors such as inventory levels, median home prices, and average days on the market provide insights into whether it's a buyer's or seller's market.

2. **Historical Price Trends**

- Analyzing historical price trends helps investors identify patterns and make informed predictions. Recognizing whether a market is experiencing upward or downward trends informs decisions on when to buy and how to negotiate.

3. **Rental Demand and Yields**

- Assessing rental demand and potential yields is crucial for the success of the BRRRR method. Markets with a high demand for rentals and favorable rental yields contribute to the overall profitability of the investment.

4. **Economic and Job Growth**

- Markets experiencing economic and job growth tend to attract more residents, leading to increased demand for housing. Investing in areas with a positive economic outlook enhances the potential for property appreciation and rental income.

Conclusion

Market research is the bedrock of successful real estate investing, especially in the *Buy* stage of the BRRRR method. Choosing the right location and analyzing market trends and demand require a comprehensive and strategic approach. Investors who diligently conduct market research position themselves for success by making informed decisions that set the stage for profitable BRRRR cycles.

Section 2: Property Selection

With a solid understanding of market research, the next pivotal step in the *Buy* stage of the BRRRR investing method is property selection. This section explores the intricacies of identifying potential investment properties and the crucial evaluation of the neighborhood and property condition. Successful BRRRR investors employ a strategic approach to property selection, ensuring that each acquisition aligns with their overall investment goals and sets the stage for a successful BRRRR cycle.

Identifying Potential Investment Properties

1. **Alignment with Investment Goals**

- The first consideration in property selection is alignment with investment goals. Each property should contribute to the investor's overall strategy, whether it's focused on rental income, property appreciation, or a combination of both.

2. **Property Type and Features**

- Understanding the target market and tenant demographic guides the selection of property type and features. Factors such as the number of bedrooms, amenities, and overall layout contribute to the property's appeal to potential tenants.

3. **Budget and Financing Considerations**

- Property selection is inherently tied to budget constraints and financing considerations. Investors must assess the affordability of potential properties, factoring in not just the purchase price but also the costs associated with renovations and refinancing.

4. **Scouting Potential Deals**

- Savvy BRRRR investors actively scout potential deals. This may involve working with real estate agents, exploring online listings, attending auctions, and networking within the real estate community to uncover opportunities that align with their investment criteria.

Evaluating the Neighborhood

1. **Neighborhood Dynamics**

- The neighborhood plays a significant role in the success of a BRRRR investment. Investors must evaluate the overall dynamics of the neighborhood, considering factors such as safety, local amenities, school quality, and community atmosphere.

2. **Market Trends and Appreciation Potential**

- Analyzing market trends at the neighborhood level is crucial. Investors should assess the historical appreciation rates in the neighborhood to gauge its potential for long-term growth and value appreciation.

3. **Tenant Demand and Rental Yields**

- The demand for rental properties in the neighborhood and the potential rental yields are key considerations. A neighborhood with high tenant demand and favorable rental yields enhances the profitability of the investment.

4. **Future Development and Infrastructure**

- Anticipating future development and infrastructure projects in the neighborhood provides insight into its growth potential. Areas undergoing positive developments may experience an increase in property values and rental demand.

Property Condition Assessment

1. **Structural Integrity**

- Assessing the structural integrity of a potential investment property is paramount. Investors should look for signs of structural issues, such as foundation cracks, water damage, or compromised structural elements, which could impact the viability of the BRRRR strategy.

2. **Renovation Potential**

- The property's potential for renovation is a critical aspect of property selection. Investors must evaluate whether the property offers opportunities for value-adding renovations that can increase its market value and rental income potential.

3. **Inspection and Due Diligence**

- Conducting a thorough property inspection and due diligence is non-negotiable. Investors should enlist the services of qualified inspectors to identify any hidden issues or necessary repairs. This information informs renovation budgets and potential challenges.

4. **Cost-Efficient Upgrades:**

- Identifying cost-efficient upgrades is essential to maximize the return on investment. Investors should prioritize renovations that add value without excessive costs, ensuring that the property remains profitable within the overall BRRRR strategy.

Conclusion

Property selection is a strategic and crucial phase in the *Buy* stage of the BRRRR investing method. Investors who master the art of identifying potential investment properties, evaluating neighborhoods, and assessing property conditions set the stage for successful BRRRR cycles.

Section 3: Financing Options

As investors navigate the *Buy* stage of the BRRRR investing method, understanding and navigating financing options are crucial components of building a successful foundation. This section delves into the exploration of different financing methods and emphasizes the importance of establishing a solid financial foundation. Successful BRRRR investors leverage various financing tools strategically, allowing them to optimize returns and position themselves for sustainable success in the competitive real estate market.

Exploring Different Financing Methods

1. **Traditional Mortgages**

- Traditional mortgages are a common financing method for real estate investments. Investors secure a mortgage from a financial institution, and the property serves as collateral. Traditional mortgages offer competitive interest rates and terms for those with strong credit profiles.

2. **Private Lenders**

- Private lenders, such as individuals or private investment firms, provide financing outside of traditional banking channels. This option can be advantageous for investors who may not qualify for traditional mortgages or seek faster approval and flexible terms.

3. **Hard Money Loans**

- Hard money loans are short-term, high-interest loans secured by the property itself. While interest rates may be higher than traditional mortgages, hard money loans offer rapid approval and are valuable for investors aiming for quick property acquisitions and renovations.

4. **Seller Financing**

- Seller financing involves the property seller acting as the lender. The investor makes payments directly to the seller, often with agreed-upon terms. Seller financing can be a flexible option for investors and may facilitate transactions that traditional financing cannot accommodate.

Importance of a Solid Financial Foundation

1. **Risk Mitigation**

- A solid financial foundation serves as a buffer against potential risks. This includes unexpected expenses, market fluctuations, or extended periods of property vacancy. Adequate financial reserves mitigate these risks and provide stability during challenging times.

2. **Flexibility in Negotiations**

- Having a solid financial foundation enhances an investor's negotiating position. Whether securing a mortgage or negotiating with private lenders, a strong financial profile instills confidence and may lead to more favorable terms.

3. **Optimizing Returns**

- A solid financial foundation allows investors to optimize returns by strategically utilizing financing. Whether leveraging low-interest traditional mortgages or high-speed hard money loans, the ability to choose the most suitable financing method contributes to overall profitability.

4. **Scalability and Portfolio Growth**

- Scalability in real estate investing hinges on a solid financial foundation. The ability to acquire multiple properties, renovate them, and repeat the BRRRR cycle relies on financial stability. A well-established financial base facilitates portfolio growth and wealth accumulation.

Conclusion

Navigating the *Buy* stage of the BRRRR investing method requires a nuanced understanding of financing options and the establishment of a solid financial foundation. Investors who explore different financing methods strategically and prioritize financial stability set the stage for successful property acquisitions and subsequent BRRRR cycles.

Section 4: Negotiation Skills

Mastering negotiation skills is a pivotal aspect of the *Buy* stage in the BRRRR investing method. In this section, we explore effective strategies for securing the best deal and building meaningful relationships with sellers and real estate agents. Successful BRRRR investors understand that negotiations extend beyond the purchase price, encompassing terms, conditions, and collaborative partnerships that set the stage for profitable BRRRR cycles.

Strategies for Getting the Best Deal

1. **Thorough Market Research**

- Informed negotiations start with thorough market research. Understanding the property's market value, recent comparable sales, and the overall dynamics of the local real estate market provides a solid foundation for negotiation.

2. **Establishing Your Maximum Purchase Price**

- Before entering negotiations, investors must establish their maximum purchase price. This figure is informed by the property's potential after renovations, expected expenses, and the desired return on investment. It serves as a non-negotiable anchor during discussions.

3. **Emphasizing Win-Win Scenarios**

- Successful negotiations create win-win scenarios for both parties. Investors should articulate the benefits of the BRRRR method, emphasizing how a quick and smooth transaction benefits the seller while ensuring a profitable project for the investor.

4. **Highlighting Quick Closings**

- Sellers often appreciate quick closings, especially those motivated to sell promptly. Investors can leverage the efficiency of the BRRRR method to assure sellers of a streamlined process, creating an additional incentive for negotiation.

Building Relationships with Sellers and Agents

1. **Open Communication**

- Establishing open communication is foundational for building relationships. Investors should communicate clearly, actively listen to the seller's needs, and express their own intentions transparently.

2. **Understanding Seller Motivations**

- Understanding the motivations behind a seller's decision to sell can inform negotiation strategies. Whether a seller is relocating, facing financial challenges, or looking for a quick sale, tailoring the negotiation approach to address these motivations enhances the likelihood of a successful deal.

3. **Building Trust and Credibility**

- Trust is a cornerstone of successful negotiations. Investors can build trust by being reliable, transparent, and demonstrating their competence in executing the BRRRR strategy. Credibility enhances the willingness of sellers to negotiate in good faith.

4. **Leveraging Real Estate Agents**

- Real estate agents play a crucial role in negotiations. Building positive relationships with agents increases the likelihood of being informed about off-market deals, gaining insights into seller motivations, and navigating negotiations with professionalism.

Conclusion

Negotiation skills are a cornerstone of successful real estate investing, and in the context of the *Buy* stage of the BRRRR method, they become paramount. Investors who master the art of negotiating not only secure the best deals on property acquisitions but also build lasting relationships that contribute to long-term success in the dynamic real estate market.

Chapter 4: Renovate - Transforming Houses into Homes

Section 1: Budgeting for Renovations

The *Renovate* stage of the BRRRR investing method marks the transformative phase where houses evolve into desirable homes. In this section, we delve into the critical aspect of budgeting for renovations. Successful BRRRR investors understand the importance of creating realistic renovation budgets and allocating funds efficiently to maximize the value of their investment properties. This strategic approach to budgeting ensures that the renovation process aligns with the investor's goals and contributes to the overall success of the BRRRR cycle.

Creating a Realistic Renovation Budget

1. **Property Assessment and Scope of Work**

- Before embarking on renovations, investors must conduct a comprehensive assessment of the property. This involves identifying necessary repairs, upgrades, and cosmetic enhancements. The scope of work serves as the foundation for creating an accurate and realistic renovation budget.

2. **Detailed Cost Estimates**

- Breakdown costs for each aspect of the renovation. This includes labor, materials, permits, and any additional expenses. Obtaining detailed cost estimates from contractors, suppliers, and service providers ensures that the budget is comprehensive and accounts for all necessary expenditures.

3. **Contingency Planning**

- Renovation projects inherently involve uncertainties. Allocating a contingency fund within the budget—typically around 10-20% of the total budget—accounts for unexpected issues or changes in the scope of work. A well-planned contingency ensures that the investor is prepared for unforeseen challenges.

4. **Market Dynamics**

- Consider the local real estate market when creating the renovation budget. Factors such as the target tenant demographic, rental rates, and property values influence the level of investment required. Aligning the renovation budget with market dynamics ensures that the property remains competitive and attractive to potential tenants.

Allocating Funds Efficiently

1. **Priority-Based Allocation**

- Prioritize renovations based on their impact on the property's value and tenant appeal. Focus on high-priority areas such as kitchens, bathrooms, and curb appeal to maximize returns. Allocating funds efficiently involves directing resources toward upgrades that yield the most significant improvements.

2. **Energy-Efficient and Sustainable Upgrades**

- Consider energy-efficient and sustainable upgrades during

renovations. While these may involve a higher upfront cost, they contribute to long-term cost savings and enhance the property's marketability. Examples include energy-efficient appliances, insulation, and sustainable landscaping.

3. **DIY vs. Professional Services**

- Assess whether certain aspects of the renovation can be completed as do-it-yourself (DIY) projects or if professional services are required. DIY tasks can save costs, but it's essential to balance savings with the need for high-quality workmanship, especially in areas that significantly impact the property's value.

4. **Long-Term Maintenance Considerations**

- Allocate funds for renovations with long-term maintenance in mind. Choosing durable materials and implementing renovations that reduce the need for frequent repairs contribute to the property's sustainability. This approach minimizes ongoing maintenance costs for the investor.

Conclusion

Budgeting for renovations is a strategic and essential aspect of the *Renovate* stage in the BRRRR investing method. Investors who create realistic renovation budgets and allocate funds efficiently position themselves for success in transforming properties into desirable homes.

Section 2: Finding Reliable Contractors

The *Renovate* stage of the BRRRR investing method involves a critical step — finding reliable contractors. In this section, we explore the intricacies of researching and selecting contractors, emphasizing the importance of ensuring quality workmanship. Successful BRRRR investors recognize that the choice of contractors profoundly influences the success of the renovation process, ultimately impacting the property's value and potential return on investment.

Researching and Selecting Contractors

1. Market Research and Recommendations

- Begin the search for reliable contractors with thorough market research. Seek recommendations from local real estate networks, fellow investors, and online platforms. Identifying contractors with a positive reputation within the community sets the foundation for a successful partnership.

2. Portfolio and Past Projects

- Assess the portfolios of potential contractors. Reviewing past projects provides insights into the contractor's style, expertise, and the types of renovations they excel at. Examining a contractor's track record helps investors align their expectations with the contractor's capabilities.

3. License and Insurance

- Ensure that contractors possess the necessary licenses and insurance. A licensed contractor has met specific requirements, demonstrating their competence and adherence to industry standards. Insurance protects both the investor and the contractor in case of unforeseen accidents or damages during the renovation.

4. References and Reviews

- Request references from past clients and read online reviews. Positive references and reviews indicate a contractor's reliability and the quality of their work. Conversely, negative feedback may highlight potential issues that investors should be aware of before entering into a contract.

Ensuring Quality Workmanship

1. **Clear Communication and Expectations**

- Establish clear communication channels and set expectations from the outset. Clearly articulate the scope of work, deadlines, and specific requirements. Open communication ensures that both parties are on the same page, minimizing misunderstandings during the renovation process.

2. **Contract and Payment Terms**

- Draft a comprehensive contract outlining all aspects of the renovation. Specify the scope of work, timeline, materials to be used, and payment terms. A well-drafted contract serves as a legal framework and provides a reference point for both the investor and the contractor throughout the renovation.

3. **Regular Inspections and Updates**

- Schedule regular inspections during the renovation process. Staying actively involved allows investors to monitor progress, address any concerns promptly, and ensure that the work aligns with the agreed-upon standards. Regular updates from the contractor foster transparency and accountability.

4. **Quality Control Measures**

- Implement quality control measures to uphold workmanship standards. This includes specifying the use of high-quality materials, conducting inspections at critical stages, and addressing any deviations from the agreed-upon plan promptly. Quality control ensures that the finished renovation meets the investor's expectations.

Conclusion

Finding reliable contractors is a crucial phase in the *Renovate* stage of the BRRRR investing method. Investors who dedicate time to thorough research, check references, and implement measures to ensure quality workmanship set the stage for successful renovations.

Section 3: Project Management

The *Renovate* stage of the BRRRR investing method not only involves finding reliable contractors but also necessitates effective project management. In this section, we explore the crucial role of overseeing the renovation process and navigating unexpected challenges. Successful BRRRR investors understand that adept project management is the linchpin for turning properties into desirable homes and ensuring the success of the entire investment cycle.

Overseeing the Renovation Process

1. **Establishing a Project Timeline**

- Develop a comprehensive project timeline that outlines each phase of the renovation. Clearly define start and end dates for specific tasks, allowing for a structured and efficient workflow. A well-thought-out timeline ensures that the renovation progresses smoothly and remains on schedule.

2. **Regular Communication with Contractors**

- Maintain open and regular communication with contractors throughout the renovation process. Establishing a feedback loop allows for immediate issue resolution, progress updates, and ensures that both parties are aligned with project goals. Effective communication fosters collaboration and minimizes misunderstandings.

3. **Budget Monitoring and Control**

- Keep a vigilant eye on the renovation budget. Regularly monitor expenses and compare them against the allocated budget. Proactive budget control helps prevent overspending, allowing investors to address financial concerns promptly and maintain the overall profitability of the BRRRR investment.

4. **Quality Assurance Inspections**

- Conduct thorough quality assurance inspections at key milestones. Assess the workmanship, adherence to the project specifications, and the use of materials. Quality inspections ensure that the renovations meet the investor's standards and align with the overall vision for the property.

Dealing with Unexpected Challenges

1. **Contingency Plans**

- Have contingency plans in place for unforeseen challenges. These can include unexpected delays, budget overruns, or issues discovered during the renovation process. Contingency plans provide a structured approach to addressing challenges and prevent them from derailing the overall project.

2. **Flexibility in Decision-Making**

- Maintain flexibility in decision-making. Unexpected challenges may require adjustments to the initial plan. Being adaptable allows investors to make informed decisions promptly, ensuring that the renovation remains on track despite unforeseen obstacles.

3. **Problem-Solving Skills**

- Cultivate strong problem-solving skills. Unforeseen challenges are inherent in renovation projects, and the ability to navigate and resolve issues efficiently is a valuable asset. Investors who approach challenges with a problem-solving mindset can mitigate the impact of unexpected events.

4. **Effective Collaboration with Contractors**

- Foster effective collaboration with contractors when challenges arise. Open communication and a collaborative approach to problem-solving strengthen the partnership between investors and contractors. Working together to find solutions ensures that challenges are addressed comprehensively.

Conclusion

Project management is a pivotal aspect of the *Renovate* stage in the BRRRR investing method. Investors who master the art of overseeing renovations effectively and navigating unexpected challenges position themselves for success in transforming properties into desirable homes.

Section 4: Adding Value to Your Property

The *Renovate* stage of the BRRRR investing method is not solely about improving aesthetics but also about strategically adding value to the property. In this section, we explore the key considerations for adding value through upgrades, emphasizing the importance of balancing cost and return on investment (ROI). Successful BRRRR investors recognize that well-planned renovations not only enhance the property's appeal but also contribute to long-term profitability.

Upgrades that Increase Property Value

1. **Kitchen Renovations**

- Kitchens often serve as the heart of a home and are a focal point for potential tenants or buyers. Upgrading appliances, installing modern cabinetry, and enhancing the overall functionality of the kitchen can significantly increase property value.

2. **Bathroom Improvements**

- Bathrooms are another critical area for renovations. Updated fixtures, modern tiling, and energy-efficient features can elevate the bathroom's appeal. Ensuring that bathrooms are clean, functional, and aesthetically pleasing adds substantial value to the property.

3. **Energy-Efficient Upgrades**

- Incorporating energy-efficient features not only attracts environmentally conscious tenants but also adds value to the property. This can include energy-efficient appliances, LED lighting, smart thermostats, and well-insulated windows. Such upgrades contribute to long-term cost savings and enhance the property's marketability.

4. **Curb Appeal Enhancements**

- First impressions matter, and curb appeal plays a pivotal role in attracting tenants or buyers. Landscaping improvements, a well-maintained exterior, and an inviting entryway can significantly increase the perceived value of the property.

Balancing Cost and Return on Investment

1. **Cost-Benefit Analysis**

- Conduct a thorough cost-benefit analysis for each planned upgrade. Assess the potential increase in property value against the cost of the renovation. Prioritize upgrades that offer a high return on investment and align with the target market's preferences.

2. **Market Research and Local Trends**

- Stay informed about local real estate trends and market preferences. Understanding what features are in demand in the local market allows investors to tailor renovations to meet tenant or buyer expectations. Aligning upgrades with market trends maximizes their impact on property value.

3. **Prioritizing Essential Repairs**

- Addressing essential repairs should be a priority. While cosmetic upgrades enhance aesthetics, ensuring that the property is structurally sound and free from major issues is crucial. Investors should allocate budget and resources to address necessary repairs before focusing on aesthetic enhancements.

4. **Long-Term Value vs. Short-Term Gains**

- Consider the long-term value of upgrades rather than solely focusing on short-term gains. While some upgrades may have an immediate impact on property value, others contribute to the property's sustainability and desirability over the long term. Striking a balance between short-term gains and long-term value is key.

Conclusion

Adding value to a property is a strategic endeavor that requires a thoughtful approach. Investors who master the art of strategic upgrades, balancing cost and return on investment, position themselves for success in the *Renovate* stage of the BRRRR investing method.

Chapter 5: Rent - Generating Passive Income

Section 1: Setting Competitive Rental Rates

The *Rent* stage in the BRRRR investing method marks the transition from property renovation to income generation. In this section, we delve into the crucial aspect of setting competitive rental rates. Successful BRRRR investors understand the significance of analyzing market rents and maximizing rental income to ensure a lucrative and sustainable return on investment.

Analyzing Market Rents

1. **Conducting Local Market Research**

- Begin by conducting thorough research on the local rental market. Analyze rental rates for similar properties in the vicinity, considering factors such as property size, amenities, and location. A comprehensive understanding of local market trends serves as the foundation for setting competitive rental rates.

2. **Comparative Market Analysis (CMA)**

- Perform a Comparative Market Analysis (CMA) to assess the rental landscape. A CMA involves comparing the property to similar rental properties in terms of size, condition, and location. This comparative approach provides valuable insights into the competitive pricing landscape.

3. **Understanding Tenant Preferences**

- Consider tenant preferences and demands within the local market. Understanding what tenants value in a rental property allows investors to tailor their offerings and set rental rates that align with tenant expectations. Features such as updated appliances, modern amenities, and proximity to essential services can influence rental value.

4. **Monitoring Rental Trends**

- Stay updated on rental trends in the area. Factors such as seasonal fluctuations, economic changes, and shifts in local demographics can impact rental rates. By monitoring trends, investors can make informed decisions on when and how to adjust rental rates to maximize income.

Maximizing Rental Income

1. **Strategic Property Marketing**

- Implement strategic marketing strategies to attract quality tenants. Highlight unique features of the property, showcase professional photographs, and leverage online platforms to reach a wider audience. Effective marketing increases the property's desirability, allowing investors to set competitive rental rates.

2. **Offering Additional Amenities**

- Consider offering additional amenities to justify higher rental rates. Upgrades such as in-unit laundry, parking spaces, or access to recreational facilities can enhance the perceived value of the property, enabling investors to command higher rents.

3. **Flexible Lease Terms**

- Explore flexible lease terms to appeal to a broader tenant base. While traditional annual leases are common, offering options for shorter leases or providing flexibility in lease terms can attract tenants who value adaptability, potentially allowing for higher rental rates.

4. **Regular Property Maintenance**

- Prioritize regular property maintenance to uphold its value. Well-maintained properties not only attract quality tenants but also allow investors to justify competitive rental rates. Tenants are often willing to pay more for a property that is in excellent condition.

Conclusion

Setting competitive rental rates is a strategic and essential aspect of the *Rent* stage in the BRRRR investing method. Investors who dedicate time to thorough market analysis, understand tenant preferences, and employ strategies to maximize rental income position themselves for success in generating passive income.

Section 2: Tenant Screening

In the *Rent* stage of the BRRRR investing method, the focus shifts to tenant screening — a pivotal step in ensuring the success of the income generation phase. This section explores the critical aspects of selecting reliable tenants and underscores the importance of thorough background checks. Successful BRRRR investors recognize that securing responsible and trustworthy tenants is essential for the sustained profitability and overall health of the investment property.

Selecting Reliable Tenants

1. **Defining Tenant Criteria**

- Clearly define criteria for desirable tenants. Consider factors such as rental history, income stability, creditworthiness, and references. Having specific criteria helps investors evaluate potential tenants consistently and objectively.

2. **Effective Property Marketing**

- Implement effective property marketing to attract the right tenant demographic. Clearly communicate property features, lease terms, and application requirements. Attracting tenants who align with the property's offerings contributes to a positive and harmonious landlord-tenant relationship.

3. **Prompt Communication**

- Prioritize prompt communication with prospective tenants. Responding to inquiries, scheduling property viewings, and addressing questions in a timely manner demonstrate professionalism. Prompt communication fosters a positive impression and sets the tone for a respectful tenant-landlord relationship.

4. **Thorough Application Process**

- Establish a thorough application process. Require prospective tenants to complete comprehensive applications, providing information on rental history, employment, income, and references. A detailed application process helps filter out candidates who may not meet the predefined criteria.

Importance of Thorough Background Checks

1. **Credit History Assessment**

- Conduct a detailed assessment of the prospective tenant's credit history. A good credit score indicates financial responsibility and the ability to meet financial obligations. Assessing credit history provides valuable insights into a tenant's financial stability.

2. **Rental History Verification**

- Verify rental history by contacting previous landlords. Inquire about the prospective tenant's payment history, adherence to lease terms, and general conduct as a tenant. Past behavior is a strong indicator of future conduct, making rental history verification crucial.

3. **Employment and Income Verification**

- Verify employment and income to ensure the tenant has a stable financial foundation. Request pay stubs, employment verification letters, or tax returns to confirm the tenant's ability to meet rental obligations. This step safeguards against potential income-related issues during the lease term.

4. **Criminal Background Checks**

- Conduct criminal background checks to assess the tenant's criminal history. This step ensures the safety and well-being of the property and surrounding community. Criminal background checks provide valuable information for making informed decisions about tenant suitability.

Conclusion

Tenant screening is a critical component of the *Rent* stage of the BRRRR investing method. Investors who master the art of selecting reliable tenants will succeed in the *Rent* stage of the BRRRR method.

Section 3: Property Management

In the *Rent* stage of the BRRRR investing method, effective property management becomes the cornerstone of successful income generation. This section explores the choices between DIY management and professional management, emphasizing the importance of handling tenant issues and maintenance. Skillful property management ensures a smooth and profitable landlord-tenant relationship, contributing to the long-term success of the investment.

DIY Management vs. Professional Management

1. **DIY Management**

Pros

- Cost Savings: Managing the property independently can save costs associated with hiring a professional property manager.
- Direct Control: Investors have direct control over decision-making, property-related tasks, and tenant interactions.
- Personal Involvement: Investors who enjoy hands-on involvement may find satisfaction in managing their properties.

Cons

- Time-Consuming: Property management requires significant time and effort, especially for tasks such as tenant communication, rent collection, and property maintenance.

- Limited Expertise: DIY managers may lack the expertise and experience that professional property managers bring to the table.
- Stress and Burnout: Handling all aspects of property management independently can lead to stress and burnout, particularly for investors with multiple properties.

2. **Professional Management**

- *Pros*
  - Time Savings: Professional property managers take on the time-consuming tasks, allowing investors to focus on other aspects of their lives or invest in additional properties.
  - Expertise: Property management professionals bring industry knowledge and experience, handling tasks efficiently and effectively.
  - Tenant Relations: Professionals can navigate tenant relations, addressing issues diplomatically and ensuring a positive landlord-tenant relationship.
- *Cons*
  - Cost: Hiring a professional property manager incurs additional costs, typically a percentage of the monthly rental income.
  - Reduced Direct Control: Investors relinquish some direct control over day-to-day property management tasks when relying on professionals.
  - Quality Varies: The quality of professional management services can vary, requiring careful selection of a reputable management company.

Handling Tenant Issues and Maintenance

1. **Effective Communication**

- Prioritize effective communication with tenants. Respond promptly to inquiries, address concerns, and maintain an open line of communication. Clear and respectful communication fosters a positive landlord-tenant relationship.

2. **Proactive Maintenance**

- Implement a proactive approach to property maintenance. Regularly inspect the property, address maintenance issues promptly, and perform necessary repairs. Proactive maintenance not only ensures tenant satisfaction but also preserves the property's value.

3. **Rent Collection Strategies**

- Establish clear rent collection strategies. Clearly communicate due dates, late fees, and payment methods. Consistent and transparent rent collection practices contribute to a smooth and predictable income stream.

4. **Conflict Resolution Skills**

- Cultivate conflict resolution skills. In the event of disputes or issues, approach conflicts diplomatically and seek amicable resolutions. Effective conflict resolution maintains a positive relationship with tenants and avoids escalation.

Conclusion

Property management is a pivotal aspect of the *Rent* stage of the BRRRR investing method. Investors who master the art of balancing DIY management and professional assistance, while effectively handling tenant issues and maintenance, set the stage for long-term success in income generation.

Section 4: Long-term Tenant Relationships

In the *Rent* stage of the BRRRR investing method, cultivating long-term tenant relationships is a strategic approach that contributes to the sustained success of the investment. This section explores effective strategies for tenant retention and creating a positive rental experience. Investors who prioritize building positive, long-term relationships with tenants position themselves for stable and predictable passive income over time.

Strategies for Tenant Retention

1. **Responsive Communication**

- Prioritize responsive communication with tenants. Address inquiries, concerns, and maintenance requests promptly. Proactive and respectful communication fosters a sense of trust and reliability, contributing to tenant satisfaction.

2. **Fair and Transparent Lease Terms**

- Establish fair and transparent lease terms. Clearly communicate rent increases, renewal options, and any changes to lease agreements. Transparent lease terms build trust and help tenants make informed decisions about renewing their leases.

3. **Regular Property Maintenance**

- Implement regular property maintenance to ensure the property remains in optimal condition. Proactive maintenance not only satisfies current tenants but also contributes to the property's overall appeal, potentially encouraging tenants to renew their leases.

4. **Incentives for Renewal**

- Offer incentives for lease renewals. This can include discounted rent for the first month of renewal, loyalty rewards, or other perks. Incentives motivate tenants to stay, fostering a positive relationship and reducing turnover.

Creating a Positive Rental Experience

1. **Responsive Property Management**

- Maintain responsive property management throughout the rental period. Address issues promptly, whether they pertain to maintenance, lease queries, or other concerns. A responsive management approach contributes to tenant satisfaction.

2. **Flexibility and Understanding**

- Demonstrate flexibility and understanding when possible. Life circumstances may change for tenants, and being accommodating within reason can strengthen the tenant-landlord relationship. This approach fosters a positive experience and increases the likelihood of lease renewals.

3. **Regular Check-Ins**

- Conduct regular check-ins with tenants to gauge their satisfaction and address any potential concerns. Actively seeking feedback and addressing issues proactively contributes to a positive rental experience and reinforces the landlord's commitment to tenant well-being.

4. **Enhanced Amenities and Services**

- Consider enhancing amenities and services. Small upgrades or additional services, such as landscaping improvements, upgraded appliances, or convenient online payment options, contribute to a positive living experience and increase tenant satisfaction.

Conclusion

Cultivating long-term tenant relationships is a strategic and essential aspect of the *Rent* stage of the BRRRR investing method. Investors who master the art of effective tenant retention strategies and create positive rental experiences position themselves for sustained success in generating passive income.

Chapter 6: Refinance - Unlocking Equity through Refinancing

Section 1: Understanding the Refinance Process

In the BRRRR investing method, the *Refinance* stage marks a pivotal stage where investors unlock equity accumulated through the initial steps of Buy, Rehab, and Rent. This section delves into the intricacies of the refinance process, emphasizing the importance of timing and providing insights into working effectively with lenders to optimize outcomes.

Importance of Timing in Refinancing

1. **Property Appreciation**

- Refinancing becomes particularly advantageous when the property experiences appreciation. Increased property value allows investors to access a higher loan amount during the refinance, providing a greater opportunity to pull out equity.

2. **Tenant Stabilization**

- Waiting until the property is fully stabilized with reliable, long-term tenants can positively impact the refinancing process. Lenders often prefer properties with consistent rental income and a history of successful tenant management.

3. **Interest Rate Environment**

- Monitoring the interest rate environment is crucial.

Refinancing during periods of lower interest rates can lead to reduced mortgage payments and improved overall financial terms.

4. **Completion of Rehab**

- It's advisable to complete the majority of the property's rehabilitation before refinancing. Lenders may assess the property's condition during the refinancing process, and a fully renovated property is more likely to appraise at a higher value.

Working with Lenders

1. **Building a Strong Relationship**

- Establishing a strong relationship with lenders is fundamental to a successful refinancing process. Regular communication, transparency, and reliability are key elements in building trust with lenders.

2. **Choosing the Right Lender**

- Selecting the right lender is critical. Consider lenders who specialize in investment properties and understand the nuances of BRRRR investing. Researching and comparing lenders based on their terms, rates, and reputation ensures a favorable refinancing experience.

3. **Understanding Loan-to-Value (LTV) Ratio**

- Loan-to-Value (LTV) ratio plays a significant role in refinancing. Lenders typically have a maximum LTV they are willing to finance. Understanding and optimizing the LTV ratio can impact the amount of equity an investor can access during the refinancing process.

4. **Gathering Necessary Documentation**

- Prepare and organize all necessary documentation before approaching lenders. This may include property appraisals, rental income history, proof of property improvements, and financial statements. Having a comprehensive and well-documented package strengthens the refinancing application.

Conclusion

Understanding the refinance process is a critical component of the *Refinance* stage of the BRRRR investing method. Investors who master the art of timing their refinancing, working effectively with lenders, and optimizing key factors such as LTV ratio position themselves for success in unlocking equity from their investment properties.

Section 2: Appraisal Considerations

In the *Refinance* stage of the BRRRR investing method, navigating the appraisal process is a critical aspect of unlocking equity from the property. This section explores the considerations surrounding property appraisal, including how to prepare for it effectively and strategies to increase the property's appraised value.

Preparing for Property Appraisal

1. **Document Property Improvements**

- Thoroughly document all improvements made to the property since its initial purchase. This includes renovations, upgrades, and any structural changes. Providing a comprehensive record of improvements helps appraisers understand the enhanced value of the property.

2. **Highlight Rental Income**

- Showcase the property's rental income history. Clearly present the consistent rental payments received and any positive trends in rental income. A stable and growing rental income history contributes to the overall attractiveness of the property in the eyes of the appraiser.

3. **Provide Comparable Sales Data**

- Research and provide data on comparable sales in the neighborhood. Identify recently sold properties with similar characteristics to demonstrate the property's competitive market value. Appraisers often consider these comparables when assessing a property's worth.

4. **Maintain Property Maintenance Records**

- Keep detailed records of property maintenance and regular upkeep. A well-maintained property reflects positively in the appraisal process. Records of routine maintenance, repairs, and upkeep activities contribute to the appraiser's perception of the property's overall condition.

Strategies to Increase Property Value

1. **Curb Appeal Enhancements**

- Invest in curb appeal enhancements to create a positive first impression. Simple landscaping, exterior improvements, and a well-maintained appearance can significantly influence the perceived value of the property.

2. **Energy Efficiency Upgrades**

- Consider energy-efficient upgrades that contribute to long-term cost savings and appeal to environmentally conscious buyers. Upgrading windows, insulation, or introducing energy-efficient appliances not only enhances the property's value but also positions it as a modern and desirable investment.

3. **Kitchen and Bathroom Renovations**

- Focus on kitchen and bathroom renovations, as these areas often have a significant impact on property value. Modern, well-designed kitchens and bathrooms are attractive to both appraisers and potential buyers, contributing to a higher appraised value.

4. **Smart Home Features**

- Incorporate smart home features to enhance the property's appeal. Smart thermostats, security systems, and integrated home automation can add a modern and tech-savvy dimension to the property, potentially increasing its perceived value.

Conclusion

Understanding the considerations surrounding property appraisal is crucial in the *Refinance* stage of the BRRRR investing method. Investors who master the art of preparing effectively for appraisal and implementing strategies to increase the property's appraised value set the stage for successful equity unlocking.

Section 3: Mortgage Terms and Options

In the *Refinance* stage of the BRRRR investing method, understanding mortgage terms and exploring different loan options are crucial steps toward successfully unlocking equity from the property. This section delves into the intricacies of mortgage terms and options, offering insights into how investors can secure favorable refinancing terms.

Exploring Different Loan Options

1. **Fixed-Rate Mortgages**

- *Definition:* Fixed-rate mortgages have a stable interest rate throughout the loan term. This provides predictability in monthly payments, making it a popular choice for investors who prefer consistent financial planning.
- *Application:* Investors seeking long-term stability and predictable payments may opt for fixed-rate mortgages. This option is advantageous in a low-interest-rate environment.

2. **Adjustable-Rate Mortgages (ARMs)**

- *Definition:* Adjustable-rate mortgages have an interest rate that may change periodically based on market conditions. Initial rates are often lower than fixed-rate mortgages but can fluctuate over time.
- *Application:* Investors willing to accept some level of interest rate variability may choose ARMs, especially if they anticipate refinancing or selling the property before potential rate increases.

3. **Interest-Only Mortgages**

- *Definition:* Interest-only mortgages allow borrowers to pay only the interest on the loan for a specified period, typically the initial years of the loan term. After this period, principal payments kick in.
- *Application:* Investors focusing on short-term cash flow may consider interest-only mortgages, as they offer lower initial payments. However, it's crucial to plan for higher payments once the principal repayment phase begins.

4. **Cash-Out Refinance**

- *Definition:* Cash-out refinance involves refinancing the property for an amount higher than the existing mortgage balance, allowing the investor to receive the difference in cash.
- *Application:* Investors looking to access a significant amount of equity for other investment opportunities or personal use may opt for a cash-out refinance. This option is suitable when property values have increased.

Securing Favorable Refinancing Terms

1. **Optimizing Loan-to-Value (LTV) Ratio**

- *Strategy:* Aim to optimize the Loan-to-Value (LTV) ratio by showcasing property improvements and highlighting its competitive market value. A lower LTV ratio enhances the likelihood of securing favorable refinancing terms.

2. **Maintaining a Healthy Credit Score**

- *Strategy:* Prioritize maintaining a healthy credit score. A higher credit score often results in lower interest rates and more favorable loan terms. Regularly monitor and address any factors that may impact creditworthiness.

3. **Demonstrating Stable Rental Income**

- *Strategy:* Provide evidence of stable rental income by showcasing consistent rental payments and a positive rental income history. Lenders often favor properties with reliable income streams.

4. **Building a Strong Relationship with the Lender**

- *Strategy:* Establishing a strong relationship with the lender is key to securing favorable terms. Clear communication, transparency, and a history of successful property management contribute to building trust with lenders.

Conclusion

Understanding mortgage terms and exploring different loan options are essential components of the *Refinance* stage of the BRRRR investing method. Investors who master the art of selecting suitable loan options and securing favorable refinancing terms set the stage for successful equity unlocking.

Section 4: Calculating Returns

Calculating returns is a critical step to gauge the success of the BRRRR cycle and make informed decisions for future investments. This section delves into the methodologies and considerations for assessing returns, providing insights on adjusting strategies for ongoing success.

Assessing the Success of the BRRRR Cycle

1. **Cash-on-Cash Return (CoC)**

- Calculate the Cash-on-Cash return, which measures the

annual return on the actual cash invested in the property. This metric considers the property's net operating income (NOI) and the initial cash investment, providing a percentage that reflects the return on investment.

- **Formula**

$$\text{CoC} = (\text{NOI} / \text{Total Cash Invested}) \times 100$$

2. **Return on Investment (ROI)**

- Assess the overall Return on Investment, which considers both cash and financing. ROI calculates the percentage return on the total investment, encompassing the initial cash investment and the financed portion.

Formula

$$\text{ROI} = (\text{Net Profit} / \text{Total Investment}) \times 100$$

3. **Equity Gain**

- Measure the equity gained through the BRRRR cycle, considering the increase in property value and equity pulled out during refinancing. Evaluating the equity gain provides a comprehensive understanding of the financial growth achieved.

Formula

$$\text{Equity Gain} = \text{Property Value} - \text{Total Investment}$$

Adjusting Strategies for Future Investments

1. **Identifying Lessons Learned**

- Reflect on the BRRRR cycle to identify lessons learned. Assess what worked well and areas that presented challenges. Understanding the nuances of each phase – Buy, Rehab, Rent, Refinance, Repeat – contributes to refining strategies for future investments.

2. **Market Analysis for Future Investments**

   - Conduct a thorough market analysis before initiating new investments. Evaluate market trends, demand for rental properties, and potential for property appreciation. A well-informed market analysis guides the selection of promising investment opportunities.

3. **Risk Mitigation Strategies**

   - Implement risk mitigation strategies based on past experiences. Identify potential challenges encountered during the BRRRR cycle and develop proactive measures to address or mitigate similar risks in future investments.

4. **Financial Goal Alignment**

   - Align future investment strategies with evolving financial goals. As financial objectives may change over time, ensure that investment strategies align with both short-term and long-term goals. This includes considerations for income generation, property appreciation, and overall financial growth.

Conclusion

Calculating returns is a pivotal step in the *Refinance* stage of the BRRRR investing method, providing investors with insights into the success of their investment cycle. By assessing Cash-on-Cash return, Return on Investment, and Equity Gain, investors gain a comprehensive understanding of the financial performance. Adjusting strategies for future investments involves reflecting on lessons learned, conducting market analyses, implementing risk mitigation strategies, and aligning investment strategies with evolving financial goals.

Chapter 7: Repeat - Multiplying Success with Multiple Properties

Section 1: Growing Your Portfolio

In the *Repeat* stage of the BRRRR investing method, the focus shifts from a singular property to growing your real estate portfolio. This section explores the strategies and considerations involved in expanding your real estate holdings and effectively managing multiple properties. Scaling a real estate portfolio requires a thoughtful approach to ensure continued success and sustained growth.

Expanding Your Real Estate Holdings

1. **Market Diversification**

- Consider diversifying your portfolio by exploring real estate opportunities in different markets. Diversification can mitigate risks associated with localized market fluctuations and economic changes. Analyze various markets, assessing factors such as demand, growth potential, and economic stability.

2. **Property Type Diversification**

- Diversify your portfolio by investing in different types of properties. This could include residential, commercial, or multi-family properties. Each property type comes with its own set of advantages and considerations. A diversified portfolio provides resilience against market-specific challenges.

3. **Financing Strategies**

- Explore different financing strategies to support the acquisition of multiple properties. This may involve leveraging existing equity, securing favorable loan terms, or utilizing creative financing options. Tailor your financing approach to align with your portfolio expansion goals and financial capabilities.

4. **Strategic Partnerships**

- Consider forming strategic partnerships to pool resources and expertise. Collaborating with other investors, real estate professionals, or even forming joint ventures can enhance your ability to take on larger projects and manage a more extensive portfolio.

Managing Multiple Properties Effectively

1. **Streamlining Operations**

- Implement systems and processes to streamline property management operations. This includes rent collection, maintenance requests, and communication with tenants. Utilizing property management software or hiring a professional property management team can enhance efficiency.

2. **Delegating Responsibilities**

- Delegate responsibilities to ensure effective management of multiple properties. If you're overseeing a growing portfolio, consider hiring property managers, maintenance personnel, or administrative staff. Delegating tasks allows you to focus on strategic decision-making and portfolio growth.

3. **Technology Integration**

- Embrace technology to facilitate property management tasks. Utilize software and tools for accounting, tenant communication, and maintenance tracking. Automation can significantly reduce the administrative burden associated with managing multiple properties.

4. **Risk Mitigation Strategies**

- Develop robust risk mitigation strategies when managing a larger portfolio. This includes having contingency plans for unexpected challenges, maintaining adequate insurance coverage, and staying informed about market trends and regulatory changes that may impact your investments.

Conclusion

Growing a real estate portfolio is a natural progression in the *Repeat* stage of the BRRRR investing method where Investors master the art of expanding their holdings and effectively managing multiple properties.

Section 2: Learning from Experience

In the *Repeat* stage of the BRRRR investing method, the journey evolves beyond the acquisition of a single property to the multiplication of success through managing multiple properties. This section delves into the importance of learning from experience, emphasizing the analysis of past investments and the continuous refinement of strategies for future success.

Analyzing Past Investments

1. **Performance Evaluation**

    - Conduct a comprehensive evaluation of the performance of each property in your portfolio. Assess key metrics such as rental income, expenses, vacancy rates, and property appreciation. Identify properties that have consistently outperformed and those that may require adjustments.

2. **Tenant and Property Management**

    - Evaluate the effectiveness of tenant and property management strategies. Analyze tenant retention rates, response times to maintenance requests, and overall tenant satisfaction. Assess property management operations to identify areas for improvement and refinement.

3. **Financial Review**

    - Review the financial aspects of each investment, including cash flow, return on investment (ROI), and financing terms. Understand the impact of financing decisions on overall profitability. Identify any financial challenges faced during the investment cycle and explore ways to mitigate them in the future.

4. **Market Trends and Conditions**

    - Stay informed about market trends and conditions that may have influenced the performance of your investments. Understand the macroeconomic factors, local market dynamics, and regulatory changes that could impact property values and rental demand.

Refining Strategies for Future Success

1. Portfolio Optimization

- Optimize your real estate portfolio based on the analysis of past investments. Consider reallocating resources, divesting underperforming properties, and acquiring assets that align with your refined investment goals. Ensure your portfolio reflects a strategic balance of risk and return.

2. Risk Mitigation Enhancements

- Enhance risk mitigation strategies based on lessons learned from past investments. Identify any unexpected challenges or risks that arose and develop proactive measures to mitigate similar issues in the future. This may include securing additional insurance coverage or implementing contingency plans.

3. Adapting to Market Changes

- Acknowledge and adapt to market changes by refining investment strategies. Markets are dynamic, and staying flexible allows you to capitalize on emerging opportunities and navigate challenges effectively. Be open to adjusting your investment approach based on shifts in the economic landscape.

4. Continuous Education

- Invest in continuous education to stay abreast of industry trends, new regulations, and innovative investment strategies. Attend workshops, seminars, and networking events to connect with industry experts and fellow investors. A commitment to learning ensures that you can apply the latest insights to your investment approach.

Conclusion

Learning from experience is a cornerstone of success in the *Repeat* stage of the BRRRR investing method. Investors who analyze past investments, refine their strategies based on lessons learned, and stay adaptable in the face of market dynamics are positioned for continuous success in managing multiple properties.

Section 3: Building a Team

In the *Repeat* stage of the BRRRR investing method, the significance of building a reliable team becomes paramount as investors grow their operations to manage multiple properties. This section explores the intricacies of assembling a network of professionals and delegating tasks for optimal efficiency, highlighting the collaborative efforts that contribute to sustained success.

Assembling a Reliable Network of Professionals

1. **Real Estate Agents**

- Collaborate with experienced real estate agents who understand the local market dynamics. A skilled real estate agent can help identify potential investment opportunities, negotiate favorable deals, and provide valuable insights into market trends.

2. **Property Managers**

- Engage professional property managers to oversee day-to-day operations. Property managers handle tasks such as tenant communication, rent collection, and maintenance requests. Their expertise ensures efficient property management, allowing investors to focus on strategic decision-making.

3. **Contractors and Renovation Teams**

- Build relationships with reliable contractors and renovation teams. Having a trusted network of professionals for property renovations is crucial for timely and cost-effective improvements. Skilled contractors contribute to the overall value enhancement of properties in the portfolio.

4. **Legal Advisors**

- Seek legal advice from professionals familiar with real estate laws and regulations. Legal advisors can assist with property transactions, lease agreements, and compliance matters. Their expertise ensures that investors navigate legal complexities and mitigate potential risks.

Delegating Tasks for Efficiency

1. **Task Assessment and Prioritization**

- Assess tasks within your real estate operations and prioritize them based on urgency and importance. Identify tasks that require specialized skills and those that can be delegated to streamline operations effectively.

2. **Roles and Responsibilities**

- Clearly define roles and responsibilities for each team member. Whether it's a property manager handling tenant relations or a contractor overseeing renovations, a well-defined scope of work ensures accountability and efficiency in task execution.

3. **Communication and Coordination**

- Establish efficient communication channels and coordination mechanisms within the team. Regular updates, meetings, and clear communication help maintain transparency and facilitate a collaborative working environment.

4. **Empowering Team Members**

- Empower team members by providing them with the resources and autonomy needed to excel in their roles. Recognize the expertise of professionals within your network and trust them to handle their assigned responsibilities. Empowered team members contribute to the overall success of the investment venture.

Conclusion

Building a reliable team is a cornerstone of success in the *Repeat* stage of the BRRRR investing method. Investors who assemble a network of professionals and delegate tasks for efficiency are better equipped to manage multiple properties and navigate the complexities of a growing real estate portfolio.

Section 4: Adapting to Market Changes

In the *Repeat* stage of the BRRRR investing method, the ability to adapt to market changes becomes paramount for sustained success. This section explores the importance of staying flexible in dynamic markets and adjusting investment strategies based on evolving economic conditions.

Staying Flexible in Dynamic Markets

1. **Market Volatility Awareness**

- Stay vigilant about market volatility and be aware of potential fluctuations in real estate markets. Understand that economic conditions, interest rates, and external factors can impact property values and rental demand. Being attuned to market dynamics allows for proactive decision-making.

2. **Monitoring Regulatory Changes**

- Keep abreast of regulatory changes that may affect real estate investments. Changes in zoning laws, tax regulations, or landlord-tenant policies can significantly impact the feasibility and profitability of investments. Regularly monitor legislative updates and adapt strategies accordingly.

3. **Evaluating Economic Indicators**

- Evaluate key economic indicators that influence real estate markets. Factors such as job growth, unemployment rates, and consumer confidence can provide insights into the overall health of the economy and, by extension, the real estate market. Use these indicators to anticipate potential shifts in market conditions.

4. **Assessing Supply and Demand Dynamics**

- Understand the supply and demand dynamics in the local market. Assess the balance between the supply of available properties and the demand from tenants or buyers. An oversupply or undersupply of properties can impact pricing and rental rates, influencing investment decisions.

Adjusting Strategies Based on Economic Conditions

1. **Flexible Financing Approaches**

- Adopt flexible financing approaches based on economic conditions. In times of economic uncertainty, securing favorable financing terms becomes crucial. Explore options such as refinancing at lower interest rates, negotiating with lenders, or leveraging alternative financing methods to optimize financial outcomes.

2. **Dynamic Property Selection Criteria**

- Adjust property selection criteria based on economic conditions. In a buyer's market, where supply exceeds demand, investors may find opportunities for strategic acquisitions. Conversely, in a seller's market, emphasis may shift towards value-added properties or those with strong income potential.

3. **Agile Renovation Strategies**

- Tailor renovation strategies to align with economic conditions. In periods of economic growth, investors might focus on value-adding renovations to capitalize on rising property values. During economic downturns, cost-effective renovations that maintain property appeal while managing expenses may be prioritized.

4. **Tenant-Centric Approaches**

- Adopt tenant-centric approaches during economic fluctuations. In challenging economic times, tenant retention becomes crucial. Implement tenant-friendly policies, consider rent adjustments based on market conditions, and prioritize effective property management to enhance tenant satisfaction.

Conclusion

Adapting to market changes is a crucial aspect of success in the *Repeat* stage of the BRRRR investing method. Investors who stay flexible in dynamic markets and adjust their strategies based on evolving economic conditions are better positioned to navigate challenges and capitalize on opportunities.

Chapter 8: Risks - Navigating Challenges in Real Estate Investing

Section 1: Market Volatility

Real estate investing, despite its potential for lucrative returns, is not without risks. In this chapter, we delve into the various challenges that investors may encounter, with a focus on *market volatility*. Understanding market fluctuations and developing effective strategies for navigating economic downturns are essential components of a robust risk management plan.

Understanding Market Fluctuations

1. **Economic Cycles**

- Real estate markets are inherently cyclical, experiencing phases of expansion, peak, contraction, and trough. Understanding these economic cycles is fundamental to anticipating market fluctuations. Investors must recognize the signs that indicate whether the market is in a growth phase, reaching its peak, contracting, or experiencing a recovery.

2. **External Factors**

- Various external factors influence market volatility. Economic indicators, geopolitical events, and changes in interest rates can significantly impact real estate markets. Investors need to stay informed about these external factors and assess their potential effects on property values, rental demand, and financing options.

3. **Supply and Demand Dynamics**

- Fluctuations in supply and demand can lead to market volatility. An oversupply of properties may result in decreased property values and increased vacancy rates, affecting rental income. Conversely, an undersupply may lead to increased competition among buyers and tenants, impacting pricing and rental rates.

4. **Investor Sentiment**

- Investor sentiment plays a crucial role in market fluctuations. Positive sentiment may lead to increased buying activity and rising property values, while negative sentiment can result in a slowdown or decline in the market. Understanding and gauging investor sentiment helps investors make informed decisions during market uncertainties.

Strategies for Navigating Economic Downturns

1. **Cash Reserves**

- Maintaining sufficient cash reserves is a prudent strategy for navigating economic downturns. Having a financial cushion allows investors to cover expenses, mortgage payments, and unforeseen challenges without being forced to sell properties at unfavorable terms. Cash reserves provide a buffer during periods of reduced cash flow.

2. **Conservative Financing**

- Adopting conservative financing practices minimizes exposure to financial risks during economic downturns. Investors should prioritize fixed-rate mortgages, which provide stability in interest payments. Avoiding excessive leverage and ensuring that financing terms align with long-term investment goals contribute to financial resilience.

3. **Diversification**

- Diversifying the real estate portfolio across different markets and property types can mitigate risks associated with localized market fluctuations. A well-diversified portfolio is less susceptible to the impact of economic downturns in specific regions or sectors, providing a more stable overall investment strategy.

4. **Proactive Property Management**

- Proactive property management is essential during economic downturns. Implementing cost-effective maintenance measures, optimizing property amenities, and employing tenant retention strategies contribute to maintaining steady rental income. Responsive property management can help investors weather challenges and position themselves for recovery.

Conclusion

Navigating market volatility is an inherent challenge in real estate investing, and understanding how to effectively manage economic downturns is crucial for investors' long-term success. The strategies outlined in this section provide a foundation for developing a resilient approach to market fluctuations.

Section 2: Property-specific Risks

Real estate investing, while rewarding, comes with its share of *property-specific* risks. This section delves into the challenges investors may face when dealing with unexpected property issues and explores effective risk mitigation strategies through due diligence.

Dealing with Unexpected Property Issues

1. **Structural Deficiencies**

   - Structural issues can pose significant challenges. Unexpected problems such as foundation cracks, roofing issues, or plumbing failures can lead to substantial repair costs. Investors must be prepared to address structural deficiencies promptly to ensure the property remains habitable and retains its value.

2. **Environmental Concerns**

   - Environmental factors, including mold, asbestos, or soil contamination, can impact property value and pose health risks. Identifying and addressing these concerns is crucial to safeguarding both the investment and the well-being of tenants. Dealing with environmental issues often involves specialized inspections and remediation efforts.

3. **Title and Ownership Disputes**

   - Title and ownership disputes can arise unexpectedly, leading to legal complications and potential financial losses. Investors must conduct thorough title searches and due diligence to ensure clear ownership rights. Addressing title issues promptly is essential to prevent delays and legal entanglements.

4. **Market Saturation**

- Market conditions can change, leading to increased competition and market saturation. An oversaturated market may result in longer vacancy periods and reduced rental income. Investors need to monitor market trends and adjust their strategies to remain competitive in dynamic real estate environments.

Risk Mitigation through Due Diligence

1. **Comprehensive Property Inspections**

- Conducting comprehensive property inspections is a fundamental aspect of due diligence. Engage qualified inspectors to assess the property's structural integrity, identify potential environmental hazards, and uncover any hidden issues. Thorough inspections provide insights that enable investors to make informed decisions before acquiring a property.

2. **Environmental Assessments**

- Environmental assessments, including mold inspections, asbestos testing, and soil analysis, are critical for identifying and addressing environmental concerns. These assessments not only protect the investment but also contribute to the overall safety and well-being of tenants. Addressing environmental issues promptly is essential for regulatory compliance and risk mitigation.

3. **Title Searches and Legal Reviews**

- Conducting thorough title searches and legal reviews is

essential to identify any existing or potential title and ownership disputes. Investors should work with legal professionals to ensure clear ownership rights and resolve any issues before finalizing a property transaction. Proactive legal due diligence minimizes the risk of legal complications down the line.

4. **Market Analysis and Research**

- Continuous market analysis and research help investors stay ahead of market saturation risks. Monitoring trends, assessing supply and demand dynamics, and understanding local market conditions enable investors to make strategic decisions. This proactive approach allows for the adjustment of rental rates, marketing strategies, and property improvements to remain competitive.

Conclusion

Navigating property-specific risks is an integral part of real estate investing, and effective risk mitigation through due diligence is paramount.

Section 3: Financing Challenges

Real estate investing involves various *financing challenges* that investors must navigate to ensure sustained success. This section explores the complexities associated with financing, focusing on managing interest rate changes and ensuring financial stability during challenging times.

Navigating Interest Rate Changes

1. **Impact of Interest Rates on Financing**

- Interest rates play a pivotal role in real estate financing. Changes in interest rates can significantly impact borrowing costs, mortgage payments, and overall profitability. Investors must stay attuned to interest rate trends and adapt their financing strategies to mitigate the effects of rate fluctuations.

2. **Fixed-rate vs. Adjustable-rate Mortgages**

- Choosing between fixed-rate and adjustable-rate mortgages is a critical decision for real estate investors. Fixed-rate mortgages offer stability with consistent interest payments, while adjustable-rate mortgages may provide initial cost savings but pose the risk of increased payments with fluctuating interest rates. Investors must assess their risk tolerance and financial goals when selecting mortgage types.

3. **Impact on Cash Flow**

- Interest rate changes can impact cash flow by influencing mortgage payments and financing costs. Rising interest rates may increase expenses, affecting profitability and the ability to service debt. Investors need to evaluate the potential impact on cash flow and adjust rental rates or investment strategies accordingly.

4. **Refinancing Considerations**

- Refinancing presents an opportunity to adjust financing terms in response to interest rate changes. However, investors must carefully consider the timing and implications of refinancing. Assessing the overall cost-effectiveness, potential savings, and impact on long-term financial stability is crucial when deciding to refinance existing mortgages.

Ensuring Financial Stability in Challenging Times

1. Maintaining Cash Reserves

- Building and maintaining cash reserves is a fundamental strategy for ensuring financial stability during challenging times. Cash reserves provide a financial cushion to cover mortgage payments, operating expenses, and unexpected challenges, reducing the risk of financial strain during economic downturns.

2. Strategic Debt Management

- Strategic debt management involves optimizing the use of leverage while ensuring that debt remains manageable. Investors should avoid excessive leverage that could lead to financial strain during challenging market conditions. Balancing debt levels with property income and overall financial health is essential for long-term stability.

3. Diversification of Investments

- Diversification of investments across different properties and markets contributes to financial stability. A well-diversified portfolio is less susceptible to the impact of localized market challenges. If one property or market faces financial difficulties, other investments may provide stability and mitigate overall risk.

4. Scenario Planning

- Scenario planning involves preparing for various economic scenarios and their potential impact on financing. Investors should conduct stress tests on their financial models, considering factors such as interest rate increases, market downturns, or unexpected expenses. Developing contingency plans enables investors to proactively address financial challenges.

Conclusion

Effectively navigating financing challenges is essential for long-term success in real estate investing. By staying attuned to interest rate changes, making strategic financing decisions, and ensuring financial stability through proactive measures, investors position themselves to thrive in the dynamic landscape of real estate investments. Prioritizing strategic debt management, diversification of investments, and scenario planning contributes to the creation of a robust and resilient real estate portfolio.

Section 4: Legal Considerations

Real estate investing is not without its *legal complexities*, and understanding and effectively navigating legal considerations are crucial for investors. This section explores the challenges associated with legal aspects, focusing on compliance with real estate regulations and handling legal issues professionally.

Compliance with Real Estate Regulations

1. **Local and Federal Regulations**

   - Real estate is subject to a myriad of regulations at both the local and federal levels. From zoning laws to fair housing regulations, investors must navigate a complex legal landscape to ensure compliance. Staying informed about the specific regulations governing real estate in each market is essential to avoid legal complications.

2. **Tenant and Landlord Laws**

   - Understanding tenant and landlord laws is paramount for real estate investors. Regulations governing lease agreements, eviction procedures, and tenant rights vary by jurisdiction. Investors must be well-versed in these laws to protect their interests, maintain positive tenant relationships, and avoid legal disputes.

3. **Environmental Regulations**

   - Environmental regulations can impact real estate transactions, particularly when dealing with properties that may have environmental concerns. Investors need to conduct thorough due diligence to identify potential environmental issues and comply with regulations related to hazardous substances, wetlands, and other environmental considerations.

4. **Financial Regulations**

- Financial regulations, including lending laws and tax codes, can significantly impact real estate investments. Investors must comply with regulations related to financing, income reporting, and property taxation. Failure to adhere to these financial regulations can lead to legal consequences and financial penalties.

Handling Legal Issues Professionally

1. **Legal Counsel**

- Engaging legal counsel is a proactive approach to managing legal considerations. Real estate attorneys specialize in the intricacies of property law and can provide invaluable guidance. Whether drafting contracts, resolving disputes, or navigating complex regulations, legal counsel ensures that investors make informed and legally sound decisions.

2. **Documentation and Contracts**

- Thorough documentation and well-crafted contracts are essential for legal protection. Investors should ensure that lease agreements, purchase contracts, and other legal documents are clear, comprehensive, and compliant with applicable laws. Detailed documentation serves as a foundation for legal protection and can mitigate risks in case of disputes.

3. **Regular Legal Audits**

- Conducting regular legal audits of real estate operations helps investors identify potential issues before they escalate. Legal audits involve reviewing leases, contracts, and operational procedures to ensure compliance with current regulations. This proactive approach minimizes the risk of legal challenges and allows for corrective action if needed.

4. **Educating Team Members**

- Educating team members about legal considerations is crucial for a cohesive and compliant real estate operation. Property managers, real estate agents, and other team members should be familiar with relevant regulations and best practices. Ongoing education ensures that the entire team operates within legal boundaries, reducing the risk of legal issues arising.

Conclusion

Legal considerations are integral to successful real estate investing, and investors must proactively manage the complexities associated with compliance and professional handling of legal issues. By staying informed about regulations, engaging legal counsel, prioritizing thorough documentation, and conducting regular legal audits, investors position themselves for a resilient and legally sound real estate portfolio. Prioritizing legal considerations contributes not only to legal compliance but also to the long-term success and sustainability of real estate investments.

Chapter 9: Scaling - Taking Your Real Estate Empire to New Heights

Section 1: Advanced Financing Strategies

As real estate investors progress in their journey, the opportunity to scale their portfolios and build a formidable real estate empire arises. This section explores advanced financing strategies that go beyond traditional methods, focusing on exploring creative financing options and leveraging other people's money to unlock new possibilities in real estate investment.

Exploring Creative Financing Options

1. **Seller Financing**

- Seller financing is a creative option where the property seller acts as the lender, allowing the buyer to make payments directly to them instead of a traditional financial institution. This arrangement can offer flexibility in terms, interest rates, and down payments, providing an alternative financing avenue for both parties.

2. **Subject-To Financing**

- Subject-to financing involves acquiring a property "subject to" the existing financing in place. In this scenario, the investor takes control of the property while leaving the seller's mortgage intact. This method allows investors to acquire properties with existing favorable financing terms without needing new financing arrangements.

3. **Wraparound Mortgages**

- A wraparound mortgage is a creative financing structure where the new mortgage "wraps around" the existing one. The buyer makes payments to the seller, who continues to make payments on the original mortgage. This strategy can be advantageous for investors looking to acquire properties with favorable existing financing while offering flexibility in the terms of the new mortgage.

4. **Equity Sharing**

- Equity sharing involves partnering with an investor or organization to fund a real estate venture. In this arrangement, both parties share in the equity, with the financing partner providing the capital, and the investor managing the property. Equity sharing can be a powerful strategy for scaling one's portfolio without the need for traditional financing.

Leveraging Other People's Money

1. **Private Lenders**

- Private lenders are individuals or entities willing to lend money for real estate investments. This option provides an alternative to traditional banks and allows investors to negotiate terms directly with the lender. Leveraging private lenders can offer faster access to capital, enabling investors to seize time-sensitive opportunities.

2. **Hard Money Loans**

- Hard money loans are short-term, high-interest loans provided by private investors or companies. While they come with higher interest rates, hard money loans offer quick access to funds, making them suitable for time-sensitive projects or opportunities where traditional financing may not be feasible.

3. **Joint Ventures**

- Joint ventures involve partnering with other investors or entities to fund and manage a real estate project. Each party brings something valuable to the partnership, whether it's capital, expertise, or resources. Joint ventures provide a collaborative approach to real estate investing, allowing investors to pool resources and share risks and rewards.

4. **Real Estate Syndication**

- Real estate syndication involves pooling funds from multiple investors to collectively invest in a real estate project. A syndicator, typically an experienced investor, manages the project, while investors contribute capital. This strategy allows individuals to participate in larger and more complex projects, leveraging the collective strength of the syndicate.

Conclusion

Scaling a real estate portfolio requires strategic thinking and innovative financing approaches. By exploring creative financing options such as seller financing, subject-to financing, wraparound mortgages, and equity sharing, investors can unlock new opportunities and optimize their capital structure.

Section 2: Diversifying Your Portfolio

Scaling a real estate empire involves more than just acquiring more properties; it requires a strategic approach to diversification. This section explores the importance of diversifying your real estate portfolio by investing in different property types and spreading risk for long-term success. While BRRRR is normally associated with single family homes, it can be applied to any type of property.

Investing in Different Property Types

1. **Residential Real Estate**

    - Residential real estate, including single-family homes, multi-family units, and apartment buildings, is a foundational component of many real estate portfolios. Investing in residential properties offers stability, a consistent demand for housing, and the potential for both short-term rental income and long-term appreciation.

2. **Commercial Real Estate**

    - Commercial real estate encompasses various property types, such as office buildings, retail spaces, and industrial facilities. Diversifying into commercial real estate provides opportunities for higher rental incomes, longer-term leases, and the potential for significant appreciation. Each commercial property type presents unique investment characteristics and risk profiles.

3. **Vacation and Short-term Rentals**

    - Vacation and short-term rentals, facilitated through platforms like Airbnb and VRBO, offer an alternative investment avenue. These properties cater to travelers seeking temporary accommodations, providing the potential for higher rental income. However, they also come with unique challenges, such as seasonality and increased management requirements.

4. **Specialized Real Estate**

- Specialized real estate includes niche markets such as student housing, senior living facilities, or medical office spaces. Investing in specialized real estate allows for targeted opportunities and unique income streams. However, it requires a deep understanding of the specific market dynamics and considerations associated with the chosen niche.

Spreading Risk for Long-term Success

1. **Market Diversification**

- Diversifying across different markets helps mitigate risks associated with localized economic downturns or market-specific challenges. Investing in properties across regions or cities allows investors to capitalize on diverse economic conditions and market trends.

2. **Income Diversification**

- Diversifying income streams within the portfolio provides stability. While rental income is a primary source, other income streams such as appreciation, tax benefits, or ancillary services contribute to a well-rounded financial picture. This approach helps safeguard against potential fluctuations in any single income source.

3. **Risk Management through Property Types**

- Different property types have varied risk profiles. While some properties may offer higher rental income, others may be more stable but with lower returns. Balancing the portfolio with a mix of property types helps manage risk and ensures a more resilient investment strategy.

4. **Adaptability to Market Changes**

- A diversified portfolio is more adaptable to market changes. Economic conditions, tenant preferences, and property trends evolve over time. A diverse portfolio allows investors to adjust their strategies based on market dynamics, ensuring resilience in the face of changing conditions.

Conclusion

Diversifying a real estate portfolio is a key strategy for investors looking to scale their empires and achieve long-term success. By strategically investing in different property types, spreading risk through market and income diversification, and maintaining adaptability to market changes, investors can create a resilient and dynamic real estate portfolio.

Section 3: Systematizing Your Processes

Scaling a real estate empire requires more than just acquiring properties; it demands the development of efficient systems and processes. This section explores the importance of systematizing your real estate investment operations, focusing on developing streamlined systems for property management and optimizing the BRRRR process for scalability.

Developing Efficient Systems for Property Management

1. **Tenant Onboarding and Offboarding**

- Establishing a systematic process for tenant onboarding and offboarding is crucial for efficient property management. This includes standardized procedures for lease signings, background checks, move-ins, and move-outs. Automation of paperwork and documentation can streamline these processes, ensuring a smooth transition for both tenants and landlords.

2. **Maintenance and Repairs**

- Efficient property maintenance and repairs are essential for tenant satisfaction and property value. Developing a system that allows tenants to report issues, scheduling regular maintenance checks, and promptly addressing repairs can prevent minor problems from escalating. Utilizing technology, such as property management software, can help track and manage maintenance requests seamlessly.

3. **Rent Collection and Financial Management**

- Establishing a streamlined system for rent collection and financial management is critical for cash flow and financial stability. Automated rent collection processes, online payment options, and organized financial tracking contribute to efficient property management. This not only saves time but also reduces the likelihood of errors or delays in financial transactions.

4. **Communication Protocols**

- Clear communication is key to successful property management. Developing standardized communication protocols for both tenants and team members ensures consistency. This may involve setting up communication channels, such as email or a property management platform, and establishing response time expectations. Effective communication fosters transparency and builds positive relationships with tenants and stakeholders.

Streamlining the BRRRR Process for Scalability

1. **Acquisition and Market Research**

   - Streamlining the acquisition phase begins with efficient market research. Utilizing data-driven tools and technologies can enhance the speed and accuracy of property analysis. Automated systems for property search, market trend analysis, and financial modeling contribute to a more efficient acquisition process.

2. **Property Analysis and Due Diligence**

   - Developing systematic approaches to property analysis and due diligence is crucial for making informed investment decisions. Standardized checklists, property inspection protocols, and digital documentation methods can streamline this phase. Automation of data gathering, such as property condition assessments and comparable property analysis, enhances the efficiency of due diligence.

3. **Renovation and Construction Management**

   - The renovation phase benefits significantly from systematic processes. Developing standardized renovation plans, contractor management systems, and quality control checklists can enhance efficiency. Utilizing project management tools and technologies helps track progress, manage budgets, and communicate effectively with contractors.

4. **Renting and Property Marketing**

- Systematizing the process of renting and property marketing is essential for minimizing vacancies. This includes developing standardized marketing materials, leveraging online platforms for property listings, and automating tenant screening processes. Efficient systems for lease signings and move-in procedures contribute to a seamless transition for new tenants.

Conclusion

Systematizing processes is a fundamental aspect of scaling a real estate empire. By developing efficient systems for property management and streamlining the BRRRR process for scalability, investors can achieve not only growth but also sustainability in their real estate endeavors. The ability to automate routine tasks, standardize procedures, and leverage technology contributes to increased efficiency, reduced operational challenges, and a solid foundation for long-term success in the dynamic world of real estate investing.

Section 4: Exit Strategies

Scaling a real estate empire involves not only acquiring and managing properties but also knowing when and how to exit strategically. This section delves into the importance of exit strategies, guiding investors on when to sell or hold properties and how to plan for retirement or venture into new opportunities.

Knowing When to Sell or Hold

1. **Market Timing**

- Understanding market cycles is crucial when deciding whether to sell or hold a property. During periods of high demand and increased property values, selling may be advantageous to capitalize on appreciation. In contrast, during market downturns, holding may be preferable to avoid selling at a loss. Regular market analysis enables investors to make informed decisions based on current market conditions.

2. **Portfolio Performance**

- Regularly assessing the performance of your real estate portfolio is key to making strategic exit decisions. Properties that consistently underperform, exhibit declining values, or have high maintenance costs may be candidates for sale. Evaluating the overall return on investment (ROI) and identifying underperforming assets allow investors to optimize their portfolio for sustained growth.

3. **Cash Flow Considerations**

- Cash flow is a critical factor in determining whether to sell or hold a property. Properties generating positive cash flow contribute to financial stability and ongoing investment opportunities. However, if a property consistently struggles to produce positive cash flow or requires significant ongoing investment, selling may be a prudent choice to reallocate resources to more profitable ventures.

4. **Tax Implications**

- Understanding the tax implications of selling or holding a property is essential for strategic decision-making. Capital gains taxes, depreciation recapture, and other tax considerations influence the overall profitability of an investment. Investors should work closely with tax professionals to assess the impact of selling on their financial position and explore tax-efficient exit strategies.

Planning for Retirement or New Ventures

1. Retirement Planning

- Real estate can be a powerful vehicle for retirement planning. Investors approaching retirement may consider selling certain properties to unlock equity for a comfortable retirement. This may involve downsizing the portfolio, selling properties with high appreciation, or utilizing 1031 exchanges to defer taxes while transitioning to a more passive investment approach.

2. Estate Planning

- For long-term wealth preservation, investors should incorporate estate planning into their exit strategies. This involves considering how real estate assets will be passed on to heirs, minimizing tax liabilities, and structuring the estate to ensure a smooth transition. Estate planning may include the creation of trusts, establishing succession plans, and making informed decisions about gifting or selling properties.

3. Venturing into New Opportunities

- Exiting certain real estate investments can provide the capital and flexibility needed to venture into new opportunities. This may involve diversifying into different asset classes, exploring emerging markets, or pursuing innovative real estate strategies. The decision to sell may align with an investor's desire for a strategic shift in their portfolio, allowing them to capitalize on evolving market trends.

4. **Risk Management**

- Exit strategies are integral to risk management in real estate. Investors should assess potential risks associated with holding a property, such as market volatility, changes in local demographics, or shifts in economic conditions. If the risk profile of a property becomes unfavorable, a well-planned exit strategy can mitigate potential losses and protect the overall health of the portfolio.

Conclusion

Exit strategies are integral to the success and longevity of a real estate empire. By understanding when to sell or hold properties, planning for retirement or new ventures, and incorporating risk management principles, investors can navigate the complexities of the real estate market with confidence. Strategic exit decisions not only optimize current portfolio performance but also position investors for future opportunities, ensuring sustained success in the ever-evolving landscape of real estate investing.

Conclusions: Celebrating Success and Looking Forward

Section 1: Reflecting on the Journey

As we reach the final chapter of this book, it's time to reflect on the transformative journey of BRRRR real estate investing. This concluding section serves as a celebration of success, providing a recap of key BRRRR concepts and sharing personal success stories from BRRRR investors who have embraced this powerful real estate investment strategy.

Recap of Key BRRRR Concepts

1. **Buy, Rehab, Rent, Refinance, Repeat**

- The BRRRR method is a dynamic real estate investing strategy comprised of five key stages. Investors begin by buying a property, then strategically rehabilitating it to enhance its value. After the renovation, the property is rented out to generate consistent income. The next step involves refinancing the property to unlock equity, and finally, the cycle repeats with the freed-up capital used for the acquisition of new properties.

2. **Leveraging OPM (Other People's Money)**

- BRRRR emphasizes the power of leveraging OPM, allowing investors to use external sources of funding to acquire and renovate properties. This includes loans, private financing, or partnerships. By utilizing OPM, investors can maximize their potential for growth without relying solely on personal capital.

3. **Forced Appreciation**

- Forced appreciation is a fundamental concept in BRRRR investing. It involves actively increasing the value of a property through strategic renovations and improvements. By implementing thoughtful and cost-effective upgrades, investors can influence the property's appraised value, enabling them to extract equity during the refinancing phase of the BRRRR cycle.

4. **Cash Flow and Passive Income**

- BRRRR investors prioritize creating positive cash flow and generating passive income from their real estate investments. Positive cash flow ensures ongoing financial stability, covering expenses and providing a steady income stream. The BRRRR strategy enables investors to build a portfolio that not only appreciates in value but also generates consistent passive income.

5. **Risk Management and Exit Strategies**

- Effective risk management is a key aspect of BRRRR investing. Investors are encouraged to understand and mitigate potential risks associated with each property. Additionally, the importance of exit strategies is emphasized, allowing investors to strategically sell or hold properties based on market conditions, portfolio performance, and personal goals.

6. **Scaling and Diversification**

- BRRRR provides a scalable approach to real estate investing, allowing investors to multiply their success by acquiring multiple properties. Diversification is also highlighted, encouraging investors to explore different property types, markets, and investment strategies to enhance the resilience of their portfolios.

Personal Success Stories from BRRRR Investors

Case Study 1: Sarah's Journey to Financial Freedom

Sarah, a determined investor, embarked on her BRRRR journey with the goal of achieving financial freedom. She started by meticulously researching her local market, identifying properties with potential for value appreciation. Sarah leveraged OPM by securing a loan to fund the initial purchase and renovation costs.

Her commitment to forced appreciation was evident in the thoughtful renovations she undertook. By upgrading kitchens, bathrooms, and enhancing curb appeal, Sarah significantly increased the value of her properties. This allowed her to refinance successfully, pulling out equity to fund additional acquisitions.

Sarah's dedication to cash flow and passive income paid off as her properties consistently generated positive returns. She carefully managed risks by staying informed about market trends and having contingency plans for unexpected challenges. As her portfolio grew, Sarah implemented exit strategies when needed, selling underperforming assets to optimize her overall returns.

Today, Sarah enjoys financial freedom and continues to scale her real estate empire. Her success story showcases the transformative potential of the BRRRR method when applied with diligence, strategic planning, and a commitment to long-term goals.

Case Study 2: Tom and Lisa's Portfolio Diversification

Tom and Lisa, a couple passionate about real estate, embraced the BRRRR strategy to diversify their investment portfolio. They recognized the importance of leveraging OPM and formed strategic partnerships to fund their acquisitions. By combining their own capital with external financing, Tom and Lisa rapidly expanded their property holdings.

Forced appreciation became a cornerstone of their approach. Tom and Lisa implemented innovative renovations that not only increased property values but also attracted high-quality tenants. This commitment to value creation allowed them to consistently refinance properties, recycling capital for new acquisitions.

Cash flow and passive income were priorities for Tom and Lisa. They implemented sound property management practices, ensuring a reliable income stream from their rental properties. By diversifying across residential and commercial real estate, they achieved a balanced portfolio that contributed to financial stability.

Tom and Lisa's success story underscores the flexibility and adaptability of the BRRRR method. Their strategic approach to scaling and diversification not only multiplied their success but also positioned them to navigate changing market conditions with confidence.

Celebrating Your BRRRR Success

As a reader, you've embarked on a journey to explore and understand the intricacies of the BRRRR real estate investing method. Whether you're a seasoned investor looking to refine your strategies or a newcomer eager to enter the world of real estate, your commitment to learning and applying these principles is commendable.

The BRRRR method is more than just a real estate strategy; it's a pathway to financial freedom, wealth creation, and a diversified investment portfolio. By reflecting on the key concepts explored in this book and drawing inspiration from real-life success stories, you're equipped with the knowledge and tools to navigate the exciting and dynamic landscape of BRRRR investing.

Looking Forward: Your Continued Journey

As you celebrate your achievements with the BRRRR method, it's essential to recognize that the journey doesn't end here. Real estate investing is a dynamic field, and successful investors are those who continually adapt, learn, and refine their strategies.

Key Takeaways for Your Continued Journey

1. **Continuous Learning**
    - Stay informed about market trends, industry changes, and evolving investment strategies. Attend seminars, engage with real estate communities, and leverage resources to expand your knowledge.
2. **Adaptability**
    - The real estate landscape is dynamic, and adaptability is crucial. Be open to adjusting your strategies based on market conditions, economic shifts, and emerging opportunities.
3. **Networking and Collaboration**
    - Building a network of like-minded investors, professionals, and mentors can provide valuable insights and support. Collaborative efforts and shared experiences contribute to ongoing success in

real estate.

4. **Innovation in Investment Strategies**
    - Explore innovative approaches to real estate investing. Stay abreast of new technologies, investment models, and market trends that may present unique opportunities for growth.
5. **Diversification and Risk Management**
    - Continue diversifying your portfolio to spread risk and enhance resilience. Regularly assess and manage potential risks associated with your properties, incorporating lessons learned from both successes and challenges.
6. **Strategic Exit Planning**
    - As your portfolio grows, strategic exit planning becomes increasingly important. Regularly assess your properties' performance and be prepared to optimize your portfolio by selling underperforming assets or capitalizing on favorable market conditions.

Your journey with the BRRRR method is a continuous evolution, marked by growth, learning, and strategic decision-making. Whether you're celebrating early successes or overcoming challenges, each step contributes to your development as a successful real estate investor.

Conclusion

As we conclude this book, take a moment to celebrate your commitment to real estate investing and the insights gained from exploring the BRRRR method. Whether you're starting your first BRRRR project or refining your existing strategies, remember that success in real estate is a journey that unfolds over time.

The BRRRR method has empowered countless investors to achieve financial freedom, create wealth, and build a diversified portfolio. As you reflect on the key concepts and draw inspiration from the success stories shared, envision the possibilities that lie ahead on your unique path in real estate.

Your continued journey is filled with opportunities for growth, innovation, and success. Embrace the challenges, stay resilient in the face of uncertainties, and remain inspired by the transformative potential of the BRRRR method.

Section 2: Encouraging Ongoing Education

As we conclude our exploration of the BRRRR real estate investing method, it's essential to recognize that education is a cornerstone of sustained success in the dynamic world of real estate. This section encourages investors to embrace ongoing education, highlighting the evolving landscape of real estate and providing valuable resources for continued learning.

The Evolving Landscape of Real Estate

Real estate is a multifaceted and continually evolving industry influenced by economic trends, technological advancements, regulatory changes, and shifts in consumer behavior. Staying informed about these dynamics is crucial for investors aiming to thrive in the ever-changing landscape of real estate. Here are key aspects to consider:

1. **Technological Advancements**

- The integration of technology is transforming various aspects of real estate, from property searches and virtual tours to data analytics and blockchain applications. Investors who embrace and leverage these technological advancements gain a competitive edge in market analysis, property management, and investment decision-making.

2. **Sustainable Practices**

- Sustainable and eco-friendly practices are gaining prominence in real estate. Investors are increasingly recognizing the value of environmentally conscious development, with green building practices and energy-efficient solutions becoming essential considerations. Staying attuned to these trends not only aligns with broader societal goals but also positions investors favorably in an environmentally conscious market.

3. **Changing Demographics**

- Demographic shifts, including urbanization, changing household structures, and generational preferences, impact the demand for various types of real estate. Investors who understand and adapt to evolving demographics can make informed decisions about property types, locations, and amenities that align with current and future market demands.

4. **Global Economic Factors**

- Global economic factors, such as interest rates, inflation, and geopolitical events, influence real estate markets. Investors need to monitor these external factors to anticipate potential impacts on property values, financing options, and overall market stability. A global perspective allows investors to navigate uncertainties and make strategic decisions in response to economic shifts.

5. **Regulatory Changes**

- Real estate is subject to evolving regulations that vary across jurisdictions. Staying informed about changes in zoning laws, tax policies, and other regulatory aspects is crucial for compliance and strategic decision-making. Investors who proactively adapt to regulatory changes can minimize risks and capitalize on emerging opportunities.

Resources for Continued Learning

1. **Industry Publications and Journals**

- Stay abreast of industry developments by regularly reading reputable publications and journals dedicated to real estate. Publications such as "The Real Estate Journal" and "Urban Land Magazine" provide in-depth insights into market trends, case studies, and expert analyses.

2. **Professional Associations and Networks**

- Joining professional associations, such as the *National Real Estate Investors Association* (NREIA) or local real estate investment groups, provides opportunities for networking and access to educational resources. Engaging with like-minded professionals fosters a collaborative environment where experiences and knowledge can be shared.

3. **Online Courses and Webinars**

- The digital age has facilitated access to online courses and webinars on various real estate topics. Platforms like *Udemy*, *Coursera*, and real estate-focused websites offer courses ranging from beginner to advanced levels. These resources enable investors to deepen their understanding of specific areas, such as market analysis, financing strategies, or property management.

4. **Seminars and Conferences**

- Attending seminars and conferences allows investors to immerse themselves in industry discussions, connect with experts, and gain exposure to emerging trends. Events like the *National Real Estate Investors Conference* or local real estate expos provide valuable opportunities for learning from seasoned professionals and expanding one's network.

5. **Podcasts and Web Series**

- Podcasts and web series offer a convenient and accessible way to stay informed while on the go. Many industry experts share their insights through engaging discussions on platforms like *BiggerPockets* podcast, *The Real Estate Guys* radio show, and *The Real Wealth Show*. Listening to these podcasts provides a wealth of knowledge and diverse perspectives.

6. **Mentorship Programs**

- Seeking mentorship from experienced investors can significantly accelerate one's learning curve. Mentorship programs, whether formal or informal, provide personalized guidance, practical advice, and real-world insights. Establishing connections with seasoned mentors can offer a unique perspective on navigating challenges and seizing opportunities.

7. **Continuing Education Courses**

- Many universities and educational institutions offer continuing education courses specifically designed for real estate professionals. These courses cover a wide range of topics, including legal aspects of real estate, investment analysis, and property valuation. Investing in formal education ensures a comprehensive understanding of key principles.

Embracing a Learning Mindset

Investors who embrace a learning mindset position themselves for long-term success. The BRRRR method introduced you to a powerful strategy, but the journey doesn't end here. The real estate landscape is vast and dynamic, offering a multitude of opportunities for growth, innovation, and continued learning.

Key Principles for Ongoing Success

1. **Curiosity and Open-mindedness**
    - Cultivate a sense of curiosity and open-mindedness. The real estate industry is diverse, and there's always something new to discover. Approach challenges with a willingness to learn and adapt your strategies based on evolving market dynamics.
2. **Networking and Collaboration**
    - Build and nurture your network. Engage with other investors, professionals, and industry experts. Collaborate on projects, attend events, and actively participate in discussions. The collective knowledge within your network can be a valuable resource.
3. **Innovation and Adaptability**
    - Embrace innovation in your approach to real estate. Stay informed about emerging technologies, market trends, and innovative investment strategies. The ability to adapt to change and integrate new ideas into your practices is a key driver of success.
4. **Continuous Evaluation and Improvement**
    - Regularly evaluate your portfolio, strategies, and performance. Identify areas for improvement and seek opportunities to refine your approach. A commitment to continuous evaluation ensures that

you remain agile and responsive to market shifts.

5. **Mentorship and Guidance**
    - Consider seeking mentorship from experienced investors who have navigated the complexities of real estate. A mentor can provide invaluable guidance, share practical insights, and serve as a source of inspiration on your journey.

Conclusion

As we conclude this book, remember that your success in real estate is not a destination but a journey. By embracing ongoing education, staying informed about industry trends, and leveraging valuable resources, you position yourself for sustained success in the ever-evolving landscape of real estate investing.

Celebrate your achievements, reflect on the lessons learned from the BRRRR method, and remain enthusiastic about the possibilities that lie ahead. The real estate journey is a continuum of growth, learning, and the pursuit of financial goals. By fostering a commitment to education, you empower yourself to navigate challenges, seize opportunities, and build a legacy of success in the dynamic world of real estate.

Inspiring the Next Generation

As we celebrate the culmination of our exploration into the BRRRR real estate investing method, this section is dedicated to inspiring the next generation of investors. It goes beyond individual success, encouraging readers to embark on their BRRRR journey and contribute to the creation of a vibrant community of successful real estate investors.

Encouraging Others to Embark on Their BRRRR Journey

1. **Sharing Your Journey**

    - One of the most powerful ways to inspire others is by sharing your own BRRRR journey. Your experiences, challenges, and triumphs can serve as a roadmap for those considering real estate investing. Be transparent about your learning process, the mistakes you've made, and the valuable lessons you've gained. Real stories resonate with aspiring investors and provide a realistic perspective on the journey ahead.

2. **Demystifying Real Estate Investing**

    - Real estate investing can sometimes seem complex or reserved for a select few. Break down these misconceptions by demystifying the process. Highlight that successful investing is attainable with dedication, education, and strategic planning. Emphasize that the BRRRR method, with its structured approach, is accessible to individuals from various backgrounds and levels of experience.

3. **Showcasing Diverse Success Stories**

    - Real estate investing is a diverse field with success stories from individuals of different ages, backgrounds, and financial starting points. Showcase a variety of success stories to demonstrate that there isn't a one-size-fits-all approach. Whether someone is a young professional, a seasoned investor, or someone looking to diversify their portfolio, BRRRR can be tailored to individual circumstances.

4. **Empowering Through Knowledge**

    - Education is a catalyst for empowerment. Encourage aspiring investors to equip themselves with knowledge before diving into real estate. Point them to valuable resources, recommend books, podcasts, and online courses that have been instrumental in your own learning journey. Empower them with the understanding that continuous learning is a lifelong pursuit in the realm of real estate.

Building a Community of Successful Real Estate Investors

1. Establishing Mentorship Programs

- Mentorship plays a pivotal role in the success of aspiring investors. Consider establishing mentorship programs within your community or participating in existing programs. Mentors can provide guidance, answer questions, and offer valuable insights. By fostering mentor-mentee relationships, you contribute to the development of a supportive and knowledgeable community.

2. Organizing Networking Events

- Networking is a fundamental aspect of real estate success. Organize or participate in networking events where investors can connect, share experiences, and build meaningful relationships. These events can range from local meetups and workshops to larger conferences that bring together investors from diverse backgrounds.

3. Collaborative Investment Ventures

- Encourage collaborative investment ventures within your community. Partnerships and joint ventures allow investors to pool resources, share expertise, and tackle larger projects.

This collaborative approach not only enhances the potential for success but also fosters a sense of community and shared accomplishment.

4. **Online Forums and Communities**

- Leverage the power of online forums and communities to create a space for discussions, Q&A sessions, and knowledge sharing. Platforms like BiggerPockets, Reddit's real estate investing community, and LinkedIn groups provide digital spaces where investors can connect, seek advice, and learn from each other.

5. **Educational Initiatives**

- Support educational initiatives that focus on real estate investing. This could involve partnering with local educational institutions, hosting workshops, or contributing to scholarship programs. By investing in education, you contribute to the growth of a knowledgeable and informed community of investors.

The Ripple Effect of Community Building

Building a community of successful real estate investors creates a ripple effect that extends beyond individual accomplishments. It fosters an environment where knowledge is shared, challenges are collectively addressed, and the journey becomes a collaborative endeavor. The benefits of community building in real estate are manifold:

1. **Shared Knowledge and Insights**

- A community provides a platform for investors to share valuable knowledge and insights. From market trends to innovative strategies, members can contribute to a collective pool of information, enhancing the overall expertise of the community.

2. **Support in Challenges**

- Real estate, like any investment, comes with its share of challenges. A community offers a support system where investors can seek advice, share their challenges, and receive guidance from those who have faced similar situations. This collective wisdom helps members navigate difficulties with confidence.

3. **Collaborative Opportunities**

- Collaborative projects and opportunities often arise within a vibrant real estate community. Whether it's a joint venture, a group investment, or a shared initiative, members can leverage each other's strengths and resources for mutual benefit.

4. **Networking and Partnerships**

- Networking is a cornerstone of success in real estate. A community facilitates networking by connecting investors, professionals, and industry experts. These connections can lead to partnerships, business opportunities, and valuable relationships that extend beyond the digital or local space.

5. **Celebration of Success**

- Celebrating successes within a community creates a positive and motivating atmosphere. From first-time property acquisitions to successful BRRRR cycles, each achievement is recognized and applauded. This culture of celebration inspires others and reinforces the belief that success is achievable through dedication and collaboration.

Inspiring the Next Generation: A Call to Action

As you reflect on your own journey with the BRRRR method, consider the impact you can have on inspiring the next generation of real estate investors. Your commitment to education, community building, and the principles of BRRRR can serve as a catalyst for positive change in the lives of aspiring investors.

A Call to Action

1. **Share Your Story**
   - Write articles, contribute to blogs, or create content that shares your BRRRR journey. Make your experiences accessible to those who are contemplating real estate investing.
2. **Participate in Mentorship**
   - Offer your expertise through mentorship programs or platforms that connect experienced investors with those seeking guidance. Be a source of inspiration and support for those navigating the complexities of real estate.
3. **Host Educational Events**
   - Organize or participate in educational events that empower aspiring investors with knowledge. Workshops, webinars, and seminars provide valuable opportunities for learning and networking.
4. **Engage in Online Communities**
   - Participate actively in online forums and communities where investors gather. Contribute to

discussions, answer questions, and share your insights. Your engagement can make a significant impact on the learning journey of others.

5. **Collaborate on Projects**
    - Explore collaborative projects within your community. Whether it's a joint investment or a shared initiative, collaboration enhances the collective strength of the community and fosters a sense of camaraderie.
6. **Support Educational Initiatives**
    - Contribute to educational initiatives that focus on real estate investing. Whether it's providing resources, sponsoring events, or offering your time as a speaker, your involvement can contribute to the growth of knowledge within the community.

Conclusion

As we conclude this book, consider the role you can play in inspiring and building a community of successful real estate investors. The impact of your actions extends far beyond individual success; it contributes to the growth, empowerment, and success of the next generation.

Embrace the opportunity to inspire others to embark on their BRRRR journey. Through sharing knowledge, fostering community, and encouraging the principles of BRRRR, you become a catalyst for positive change in the realm of real estate investing. Celebrate your achievements, and with enthusiasm and dedication, look forward to the exciting possibilities that lie ahead for both you and the aspiring investors you inspire.

Section 4: Final Words of Advice

As we reach the final section of this book, it's time to offer some parting words of advice for future BRRRR investors. This section aims to encapsulate the wisdom gained from the exploration of the BRRRR method and inspire a mindset of lifelong growth and financial success.

Words of Wisdom for Future BRRRR Investors

1. **Start with Education**

- "Knowledge is the key to success in real estate investing. Before you embark on your BRRRR journey, invest time in educating yourself. Learn about market trends, financing options, and the intricacies of the BRRRR method. A well-informed investor is better equipped to make strategic decisions and navigate challenges."

2. **Patience is a Virtue**

- "Real estate is a long-term game, and patience is a virtue. The BRRRR method unfolds over multiple stages, from buying and renovating to renting and repeating. Embrace the process and understand that each step contributes to the overall success of your investment strategy. Patience allows you to weather uncertainties and make informed decisions."

3. **Build a Strong Network**

- "Your network is a powerful asset in real estate. Surround yourself with like-minded individuals, professionals, and mentors who can offer guidance and support. Collaborate on projects, share experiences, and learn from the collective wisdom of your network. Building strong relationships is a cornerstone of success."

4. **Embrace Challenges as Opportunities**

- "Challenges are inevitable in real estate, but they also present opportunities for growth. When faced with obstacles, view them as opportunities to learn, innovate, and refine your strategies. Overcoming challenges contributes to your resilience as an investor and positions you for long-term success."

5. **Diversify Strategically**

- "Diversification is a key principle in investment strategy. As you grow your real estate portfolio, consider diversifying strategically. Explore different property types, markets, and financing options. Diversification minimizes risk and enhances your ability to adapt to changing market conditions."

6. **Adaptability is Essential**

- "The real estate landscape is dynamic, and adaptability is essential for success. Be open to adjusting your strategies based on market trends, economic shifts, and emerging opportunities. Embrace innovation, stay informed about industry changes, and position yourself as an adaptable investor."

7. **Continuously Evaluate and Improve**

- "Regularly evaluate your portfolio, investment strategies, and performance. Identify areas for improvement and be proactive in refining your approach. Continuous evaluation ensures that you remain agile, responsive to market shifts, and consistently strive for excellence in your real estate endeavors."

8. **Celebrate Achievements, Learn from Mistakes**

- "Celebrate your achievements, no matter how small, and learn from your mistakes. Both successes and challenges are integral parts of the real estate journey. Reflect on your experiences, analyze outcomes, and use them as stepping stones for continuous improvement."

9. **Leverage the Power of Compound Growth**

- "The BRRRR method is not just a one-time strategy; it's a pathway to compound growth. Leverage the power of compounding by reinvesting the returns from each cycle into new opportunities. Over time, compounding accelerates your wealth-building journey and sets the stage for financial success."

10. **Stay Committed to Lifelong Learning**

- "Realize that the journey of real estate investing is a continuum of learning. Stay committed to lifelong learning, staying informed about market trends, and continuously expanding your knowledge. The more you learn, the more you empower yourself to make informed decisions and seize opportunities."

Embracing a Lifelong Mindset of Growth and Financial Success

1. **The Journey Never Ends**

- "Realize that success in real estate is not a destination; it's a continuous journey. Embrace the mindset that your journey as a BRRRR investor is ongoing. The challenges you overcome, the lessons you learn, and the successes you achieve contribute to your growth as an investor."

2. **Cultivate a Growth Mindset**

- "Cultivate a growth mindset that thrives on challenges and sees failures as opportunities for improvement. A growth mindset fosters resilience, adaptability, and a proactive approach to navigating the complexities of real estate investing."

3. **Seize Opportunities with Confidence**

- "As you continue your journey, seize opportunities with confidence. Trust in the knowledge you've gained, the strategies you've refined, and the resilience you've developed. Each opportunity is a chance to apply your skills, contribute to your success, and move closer to your financial goals."

4. **Inspire Others Along the Way**

- "As you progress, consider the impact you can have on inspiring others. Share your experiences, offer guidance, and contribute to the development of a supportive community. Inspiring others creates a positive ripple effect that strengthens the fabric of the real estate investing landscape."

5. **Celebrate Milestones and Reflect**

- "Celebrate milestones along the way and take moments to

reflect on your achievements. Whether it's completing a successful BRRRR cycle, acquiring a new property, or reaching a financial milestone, acknowledge your progress. Celebration reinforces your commitment and motivates you for future endeavors."

6. **Contribute to the Industry**

- "Consider contributing to the real estate industry in meaningful ways. Whether it's through mentorship, educational initiatives, or collaborative projects, your contributions enrich the collective knowledge and success of the community. Your impact extends beyond individual achievements to shaping the industry's future."

Final Thoughts

As you embark on your BRRRR journey or continue refining your strategies, remember that the journey is a testament to your dedication, resilience, and commitment to financial success. The BRRRR method is more than a technique; it's a transformative approach to real estate investing that can shape your financial future.

May your future endeavors be marked by growth, prosperity, and the fulfillment of your financial goals. Embrace the lessons learned, celebrate your achievements, and look forward to the exciting possibilities that lie ahead. The world of real estate investing is dynamic, and with a mindset of continuous learning and strategic decision-making, you position yourself for success in the ever-evolving landscape of BRRRR real estate investing.

Here's to your ongoing growth, financial success, and the next chapter in your BRRRR journey!

Good luck.

Check out WWW.JIMPELLERIN.COM[1] for more articles on Real Estate Investing.

1. http://WWW.JIMPELLERIN.COM

About The Author

JIM PELLERIN started real estate investing over twenty years ago. Since then, he has bought and sold millions of dollars of real estate. He began by purchasing and renting out duplexes. Recently he has added Lease Options to his strategy. He is currently acquiring two to four Lease Option properties a month. He has implemented many unique funding strategies that have allowed him to continue implementing his strategy and continue building his sizable portfolio.

As part of his education, he has attended numerous seminars on real estate investing, project management, property management, financing, renovations, motivation, time management, and many more. He has also read over 500 books on similar topics.

This book blends his experience and the knowledge he has gained through his investments and studies.

Visit his author page to discover my other publications: books2read.com/JimPellerin[1]

1. https://books2read.com/JimPellerin

Other Books By Jim Pellerin

Real Estate Investing: Strategies – The Secret to Financial Independence with Real Estate

books2read.com/strategies[1]

1. https://books2read.com/strategies

Real Estate Investing with Lease Options – How to Invest with No Money Down

books2read.com/Lease-Options[2]

2. https://books2read.com/Lease-Options

Invest NOW – The Passive Approach to Winning with Real Estate

books2read.com/investnow[3]

3. https://books2read.com/investnow

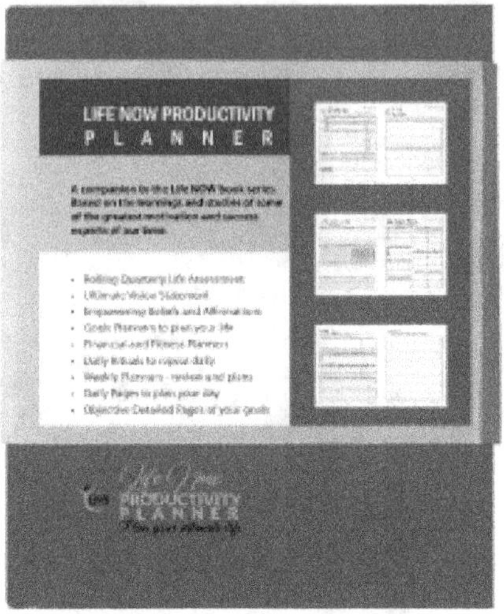

books2read.com/JimPellerin[4]

4. https://books2read.com/JimPellerin

Don't miss out!

Visit the website below and you can sign up to receive emails whenever Jim Pellerin publishes a new book. There's no charge and no obligation.

https://books2read.com/r/B-A-WGIX-DIZXC

BOOKS2READ

Connecting independent readers to independent writers.

Did you love *Unleashing Wealth: A Guide to BRRRR Real Estate Investing*? Then you should read *Real Estate Investing Strategies: The Secret to Financial Independence with Real Estate*[5] by Jim Pellerin!

[6]

The mechanics of Real Estate Investing is simple: Buy a house and do something with it. Fix it and rent it, or just sell it. Sounds simple, doesn't it? Yet only a small percentage of us have enough courage to go out and take advantage of the opportunities that are available to us. Real Estate Investing can be more promising than stocks, bonds, and various other securities because of the higher rates of return.

In this book, I show you how to get started by describing the different types of skills you need, by showing you how to take control of your personal and financial situation, and by helping you decide what type of real estate investing you want to get involved in. I also show

5. https://books2read.com/u/m2QyNG

6. https://books2read.com/u/m2QyNG

you how to find properties, how to analyze them, and how to make an offer that makes sense. And finally, I describe what you need to do to manage your investment and ultimately how to sell your investment for the most profit.

I have been involved in real estate investing for over 20 years. I have yet to find a book that focuses on the investor and the overall process. Sure, there are lots of books on fix and flips, buy, rent and hold, rent to own, etc. However, I haven't found any good books on how to really get started in the real estate investing process from a practical viewpoint. The technical aspects of real estate investing are really quite easy. But if it's so easy, then why isn't everyone doing it?

This book is for people who are serious about getting started in real estate investing and who want to join the 5% of those who actually take action and invest. This book provides a strategic approach with the tried and tested methods and principles that have helped others make millions in real estate.

Read more at www.jimpellerin.com.

Also by Jim Pellerin

Real Estate Investing

Real Estate Investing Strategies: The Secret to Financial Independence with Real Estate

Real Estate Investing with Lease Options - Investing in Real Estate with No Money Down

Invest Now - The Passive Approach to Winning at Real Estate

The Ultimate Beginners Guide to Real Estate Investing

The 98 Best Real Estate Investing Strategies

The Ultimate Beginners Guide to Wholesale Real Estate Investing

The Ultimate Beginners Guide to Rental Real Estate Investing

The Ultimate Beginners Guide to Fix and Flip Real Estate Investing

The Ultimate Beginners Guide to Private Equity Real Estate Investing

Ultimate Beginners Guide to Real Estate Investing Financing

Building Wealth Through Real Estate - A Beginners Retirement Guide

The Ultimate Guide to Marketing for Real Estate Investors

Unleashing Wealth: A Guide to BRRRR Real Estate Investing

Watch for more at www.jimpellerin.com.

About the Author

Jim Pellerin has been investing in Real Estate for over 25 years. During that time, he has conducted over $30M worth of real estate transactions.

He was the founder of several Real Estate businesses with the latest, Peller Media, focusing on providing digital marketing services for real estate professionals such as real estate agents and mortgage brokers and investors.

He has read over 700 books on subjects such as real estate investing, self development, education, cognitive psychology, marketing and sales.

He has a degree in Computer Science which he received from the University of New Brunswick in Fredericton, New Brunswick, Canada.

Read more at www.jimpellerin.com.

www.ingramcontent.com/pod-product-compliance
Lightning Source LLC
LaVergne TN
LVHW050302210926
848481LV00014BA/802